BUY REAL ESTATE WITHOUT CASH OR GOOD CREDIT

A Bootstrapper's Guide

I'll show you how I built wealth through real estate — and how you can start today regardless of your finances.

GERALD HONEYBLUE

Table of Contents

DEDICATION

This book is dedicated to the memory of my parents:
James Willie and Erma Honeyblue

My mother always said, "everybody's got a sermon in them and a book in them" my father, "everybody's got a business in them."

Both of my parents are now deceased. My father passed in 1997, and my mother passed in 2024 before this book was completed so regretfully, she never got a chance to see it.

I grew up watching my father juggle a day job and a series of side hustles. From selling firewood to repairing boats and hauling junk, he always had his 5-to-9 going. Over the years, I realized it was this commitment to hard work after hours that truly brought out the bootstrapper in him. He continued this pattern until he was around 40 when he finally pursued his dream full-time by starting a logging business that ultimately became very successful.

As a child, I often wondered why he worked so much and so hard. It wasn't until I got older that I understood his two main motivations: (1) he was determined to create generational wealth for our family, and (2) it was in his DNA to "do for self" and always have something of his own. Without a doubt, he was the most determined person I've ever met. He had enough drive and determination to move a mountain!

My father believed in education but he himself never graduated high school. He sent five of the seven us to college. I vividly recall him telling us that we needed to get a good education, not just schooling but we also needed to develop some skills that we could do with our hands.

After watching my father work hard most of his life, I vowed to go to school, get a good education, and find a stable job so I could live comfortably without the need to hustle on the side. I did earn a good education and found a solid job, but I still found myself side-hustling. Believe it or not, my "WHY" is the same as my father's, to build generational wealth, to have my own, and to "do for self." I am here to tell you folks if you didn't know, DNA is powerful as heck! You can't outrun it, you can't hide from it or even conceal it, particularly if you're in an environment that nurtures it. That DNA will eventually kick in!

I gained much of my construction knowledge from my father while building our own house from the ground up. He bought materials each week when he got paid and we spent nights and weekends building that house. I was a young teenager at the time and the last thing I wanted to do was to spend my nights and weekends working on a stinking house. I wanted to hang out and enjoy myself like most other young teenagers. I vividly recall my father saying, "son, you need to learn this stuff, you're going to need to know it one day." And I recall saying to myself that "I will never have to work on another house; I'm going to be able to pay somebody to do that kind of work for me." But as always, he knew best. Little did I know at the time; the groundwork had already been laid. What do you think I have been doing with my nights and weekends for the last 20 years? You guessed it – working on old houses, and it's been a labor of love! Thanks Dad!

ACKNOWLEDGMENTS

I would like to thank those around me who helped make this book project possible. This book started as a 90-day project and has morphed into a nearly two-year-long labor of love. I should have known from the start that it would take me much longer than 90 days. I refuse to put something out there just so I can say that I have written a book. Also, I'm the kind of person who, if you ask me what time it is, will end up teaching you how to build a timepiece. So let me be clear—this is the absolute best I have to offer you!

I would like to thank my wife Virginia for 40-plus years of love, marriage, and dedication. We met in college as two broke, first-generation college students. She became the love of my life, and the rest is history.

Virginia is one of the most dedicated hard-working people that I've ever met. She has done a tremendous job of supporting me throughout the years and raising our family. While researching this book, I realized that I had been working 70 to 90 hours per week for over 30 years. I worked a full-time job while also running two separate businesses.

What I didn't realize was that Virginia was also working a full-time job with a 1.5-hour commute each way. She was always awake when I went to bed and up before me each morning. She raised our daughter, managed the household, and ensured we had a sit-down family dinner every night. In every way, she put in more hours than I did.

I'd like to thank my daughter, Shamika Honeyblue-Keel. We both consider ourselves as each other's biggest cheerleaders. She has been a pleasure to raise and will always be *my little girl*, regardless of her age and stature. We're so proud that she has become such a charming young lady and an accomplished professional.

Shamika has always been wise for her years and served as my editor for this project, counselor, and voice of reason throughout my real estate investing career. I would immediately call her to debrief after every real estate guru seminar. She would listen intently and dissect all the information, then calmly and tactfully remind me not to chase the shiny object and stay focused on my real estate goals.

Next, I would like to recognize three of my mentors, starting with Edward Littlejohn of Steubenville, Ohio. Ed is a Real Estate Investor, Entrepreneur, Businessman, and accomplished Martial Arts Instructor. His demeanor and inner calm make him very easy to talk with and bounce ideas off. It is true that when the student is ready, the teacher will appear. Ed and his wife, Vicki, are a shining example of how to meld family and business to solidify a legacy for future generations.

Stephen Van Cauwenbergh of Oklahoma City, OK, is a real estate investor, entrepreneur, and businessman. He has been a source of inspiration, overcoming numerous challenges with resilience and determination. He has overcome situations that would have caused most people to just quit and give up. He truly started with nothing and created something in the real estate world. Steve has used real estate to fund several successful business ventures in Oklahoma. I still subscribe to Steve's philosophy of "just go buy assets."

Finally, I would like to thank Jeffrey Taylor, "Mr. Landlord," of Chesapeake, Virginia. It's through Jeffrey and his teachings that I found true wealth in real estate. I had traveled throughout the country chasing over 50 real estate gurus. They taught me how to buy properties without cash or good credit. But it's through his teaching and education program that I developed a mindset of running my real estate business like a business. Jeffrey believes in developing systems and numerous ways to do everything in the property management business. Jeffrey and his wife, Dot, run their education business and provide outstanding training on property management.

An honorable mention goes out to Lin Phelps, who connected me with my editor, Kimberly Meadows of Write Touch Publications. Kim did an awesome job of taking my ragged thoughts and shaping them into a work of art that I'm now proud to present to the world. Others that I would like to recognize are Kenneth Roberts, Myrick Peacock, Sean Keel, Al Williamson, Cedric Russell, Myra Rice, AC Johnson, Marcell Umphrey, and Andrew Knott.

INTRODUCTION

I am truly honored that you've purchased this real estate investment book. My goal in writing it is twofold:

1. To answer the most frequently asked question: *"Can you really buy real estate even if you have no money or bad credit?"* The short answer is yes—even if you're broke and have bad credit, investing in real estate is possible.
2. I want to provide you with the confidence and inspiration to turn off the television, get off the couch, and secure your first property at a significant discount. Ideally, the techniques in this book will not only help you acquire property but also guide you toward building wealth—potentially even millions—through real estate investment.

I consider this book a bootstrapper's guide, rooted in my own experiences. To me, bootstrapping means starting where you are with what you have. It's a great way to get started, but at some point, you must legitimize your business. Constantly restarting every Monday morning isn't building a business, it's just a hustle. While hustling is fine in the beginning, you don't want to spend your entire life stuck in that cycle. The goal is to grow beyond bootstrapping and create something sustainable. Let's face it: we all must have a place to live. By applying just one technique from this book to purchase a home for as little as 50 cents on the dollar or less, you could save tens or possibly hundreds of thousands of dollars in mortgage payments and interest over the life of a typical mortgage loan.

If you operate a business, you will need a place to conduct it. Therefore, we are all investing in real estate in one way or another. The difference is that some of us invest in our own properties and build generational wealth, while others pay rent and invest in their landlord's dreams.

I'm taking you on this journey with me, but first, let me explain how this book is structured. Some sections will read like a textbook, recipe book, or how-to guide. But don't worry, I've included a glossary at the end to clarify industry jargon. If you come across an unfamiliar term, just flip to the back for a quick definition. A large portion of the book is dedicated to inspiration. I firmly believe that real estate investing, just like any other entrepreneurship endeavor can be a lonely business, especially when you are not closing deals and making money despite all your marketing efforts. In short, you are spending money on your business and not making any money.

I chronicle several deals I've completed over the years, many with little to no money. I'll break down how I found each deal and provide relevant details, linking them to the techniques discussed in each section. Some deals are included simply to "spice things up," but every deal shared is one I have personally done. Most of the strategies in this book are ones I've used myself. If I discuss a technique I haven't personally tried, I'll be upfront about it.

I encourage you to keep an open mind and embrace the techniques I'm about to share. By the way, having, someone to accompany you on this journey— whether it's a spouse, friend, family member, acquaintance, or any like-minded individual—can make the process much easier.

Often, the loneliest part of this business is when you are diligently marketing and doing all the right things but can't seem to close a deal. Even when you and the seller agree on price and terms, deals can still fall apart for countless reasons. The seller might back out due to their attorney's advice, accept a better offer, or run into ownership title issues—the list goes on. But don't worry—I'll share insights to help you improve your chances of finding great deals and successfully closing them.

Of course, we know that the most exciting time in this business is when you are sitting at the closing table, and the attorney hands you that big check. For me, it's a feeling like no other feeling I've had in business. I still get excited, so excited that I want to take every check, frame it, and share it with the world.

I encourage you to let everyone around you know that you are about to embark on your real estate journey and invite them to join you—provided they are willing to put in work and invest in themselves first. I want you to FIND your passion in real estate or FUND your passion through real estate.

My Story

Real estate has been incredibly rewarding for me over the past 25+ years of investing. It has allowed me to retire with dignity from my good government job, travel to destinations that I normally would not have visited and form lifelong friendships with like-minded real estate investors.

In those 25-plus years, I have been involved in dozens of real estate transactions of my own and many more alongside students. I use the term "students" loosely, as I'm often reminded that I've never been paid for teaching, mentoring, coaching, or guiding new investors to the closing table. I would literally accept anyone who showed up at our meetings and coached them to complete their first real estate deal. Watching students' faces light up when they receive that big check at the closing table has always been a thrill for me. A few of my students have amassed tremendous wealth investing in real estate. Most of them still reach out—whether by call, text, or email—whenever they have questions about a deal, even today.

I'm guessing you did not pick up this book to read about the deals that I bought with 20 percent down and bank financing because of my 800-plus credit score. I've done those, but those deals are not as fascinating to read about, especially if you're seeking real estate education, and inspiration and looking to get started with no money.

Instead, I will take you on my journey and provide a few tips to keep you motivated in this business. We will cover some of my life lessons, including both my losses and my successful deals. For instance, I'll tell you about the house I bought that had over a million dollars in liens on it, the one I purchased with what I jokingly call "cigarette money," and the cheapest house I ever bought. While I can't possibly cover every deal I've done over the years, I'll dive deep into a few notable ones and sprinkle in some nuggets of wisdom that even seasoned investors can benefit from.

The good deals are out there but you must be committed to looking and digging where others refuse to look and dig. Your local courthouse and the legal section of your local newspaper should become your new best friends—but more on that later.

Chapter 1:

HOW I STARTED

I refer to myself as the "bootstrapping real estate investor" because I built my real estate investment wealth from the ground up. I happen to be a third-generation bootstrapper, following in the footsteps of my entrepreneurial father and grandfather. Growing up, I watched my father start with nothing, yet he successfully built a thriving logging business that supported a family of seven children. My grandfather, the original bootstrapper, was born before the turn of the century. Despite the many challenges, he created his legacy by buying a farm. My grandfather raised his family on that farm, which remains in our family today—over 120 years and five generations later.

I believe entrepreneurship and a do-it-yourself mindset are in my DNA. Even when it requires unorthodox methods, I've always embraced a hands-on approach. When I say "unorthodox," I mean that many of my ventures began as side hustles, often with little or no capital—just a vision, a plan, focus, and a lot of hard work. The lessons learned from taking an "L" (Loss) left an indelible impression on me as an example of what not to do next time. It's like touching a hot stove for the first time. That burn is so unforgiving that it leaves blisters and sometimes permanent scars, constantly reminding you of what not to do again.

A close friend of mine, who was both an entrepreneur and mentor during my vending business days, had a similar mindset. He would purchase inventory and travel across the country to attend weeklong events where he sold his products. Most of the time, he did well, but occasionally, there were events where sales were so poor that he barely earned enough for gas to get back home. After one of those rough weeks, I was talking to him and asked him how he felt about spending money on inventory, travel, and lodging, only to return home broke. His response has always stuck with me: "I don't view it as failing. I view it as very expensive tuition."

Chances are, you too might fail at your first business/side hustle, especially if it's undercapitalized. But go ahead, get your failures out of the way. Embrace the failures as learning opportunities, keep moving forward with a solid plan and you will eventually succeed. I promise you!

MY EARLY YEARS

I have always had a burning desire to have my own and control my own destiny. That must be the bootstrapper in me. I just always wanted to make my own money. Ever since I can remember, we would return drink bottles to the store for the three-cent bottle deposit. Back then, soft drink companies would buy back empty bottles, which were washed and refilled. Stores gladly accepted discarded bottles and sent them back to the bottling companies.

We often found these bottles in ditches along the roadside, and it became a small but exciting source of income.

That was probably my earliest venture into entrepreneurship. We also collected scrap copper, aluminum, and other metals from the county landfill. We took the scrap metal to a scrap metal recycling yard and sold it by the pound. They generally paid us pennies per pound, which was more than enough for snacks and drinks at that time.

I think I started working for someone else around the age of 7 or 8. Initially, we worked in the fields pulling weeds, and as I got older, I started chopping weeds in the peanut fields with the adults. I worked on the farm every summer until I was 15. That summer, I landed a government-sponsored job as a carpenter's helper at my high school, working for my shop teacher. Although I had to walk a mile to and from work each day, I was thrilled to have a job that required skill and paid a decent hourly wage. Plus, it got me out of the hot sun and the backbreaking fieldwork.

My other summer jobs included harvesting truck crops, cucumbers, corn, beans, tobacco, watermelons, cantaloupes, you name it. It was that grueling work in the hot sun that convinced me that I needed to go to school and get a good education. I am content to leave that hard labor to someone else.

Please don't get me wrong. You would think that having grown up in rural eastern North Carolina in the 1960s, I would have been raised in abject poverty. My parents provided the basics for us: food, shelter, and clothing. If we wanted fancy clothes or the latest gadgets, we had to go out and earn the money to buy those things.

I vividly remember wanting a pair of Converse tennis shoes—you know the ones with the star on the side. Those tennis shoes cost a whopping $10.00 back then. That was a lot of money in the late 1960s when the minimum wage was just $1.65 per hour. At that time, we were earning $3.50 per day for chopping in the peanut fields. The prevailing wage for chopping peanuts at the time was $7.00 for adults. Since we were children, we were paid half the adult rate. We worked from 7:00 AM to 6 PM, with a one-hour lunch break at noon, totaling a full ten hours each day under the hot sun at 35 cents per hour.

Now, back to the tennis shoes! My parents would buy us the cheaper tennis shoes from the local Dime Store, which cost only $1.99. These shoes were so cheap they didn't even come in a box; they were packaged in a clear plastic bag. Needless to say, they weren't the kind that promised to make you "run faster and jump higher." I wanted the more expensive pair, so I had to buy them myself. But even as a child, I could not justify spending the equivalent of three days' wages on a pair of tennis shoes. So, I compromised and bought a $6.00 pair of Pro Keds—you know, the ones with the red and blue stripe on the side of the sole? Honestly, I think those shoes really did make me run faster and jump higher!

MY ADULT YEARS

I think my first true solo money-making entrepreneur venture started while in college. I used to tutor classmates in drafting and assist them in their drafting projects. At the time, I didn't consider drafting as work because I loved it so much. Drawing was something that I was good at, and I thoroughly enjoyed it, so I didn't view it as a job or think of myself as an entrepreneur. Looking back now, though, I realize that drafting was my first official business, my first solo side hustle.

Since then, I've started several side hustles, all in true boot-strapper fashion—without much capital. One of my earliest ventures was buying and reselling items from mini storage auctions. I was buying and selling in the early 1980s, long before the popularity of the reality television shows that we see today. Believe me, today's television shows are far from reality. I once watched a television show where someone paid $300 for a storage unit and found a $50,000 vintage automobile hidden beneath the junk and debris. That's all Hollywood!

Our state General Statutes require that storage unit auctions be listed in the legal section of the newspaper when people fail to pay their rent. Usually, only a handful of bidders showed up, and the stuff was always sold cheap because the auctioneers mainly just wanted the units cleaned out. I bought enough furniture to furnish the entire living room in my first house for less than $10.00. There were just incredible deals to be found at that time.

I focused on buying used books cheaply and reselling them to a local used bookstore. Imagine that—I was selling used books in 1984, a full decade before Jeff Bezos started Amazon!

I ventured into multi-level marketing (MLM) on three different occasions, selling products directly to family, friends, and acquaintances. My first experience was with a well-known company that built its reputation selling soap, detergent, and cleaning products. Later, I also dabbled in a few others, selling health supplements and legal services. People tend to shy away from MLM due to its negative connotations. It's understandable—because you never actually own a business, and you are always chasing someone else's dream. But some of the positives found in MLM are that:

- It allows you to start a business cheaply, sometimes less than a hundred dollars.
- In the eyes of the IRS, you are now in business and qualify for business tax deductions, which could reduce your income tax.
- They will teach you their business systems, help you understand business, and help you develop your sales and presentation skills.
- It allows you to operate with a group of like-minded individuals, and they will definitely keep you motivated and pumped up.

After my experiences with MLM, I spent several years working in the flea market circuit, where I could rent a space every weekend for as little as $5.00 a day. I sold a range of items, from used work uniforms, neckties, household items, and t-shirts. The experience inspired me to start my most profitable side business, printing t-shirts and other garments. I started out with a heat press that I used to iron designs on shirts, caps, and other garments. Eventually, I expanded, purchasing a screen-printing system and growing my operation. I ran that printing business out of my garage for more than 20 years before selling the business and its equipment.

Like my father, who bootstrapped his logging business, I bootstrapped my printing business. He believed in owning all his equipment outright to reduce overhead and avoid monthly equipment payments. I located good used equipment and paid cash for it. The t-shirt business is seasonal, so paying cash allowed me to eliminate monthly payments and reduce my monthly obligations. As a result, I could afford to shut down for the winter season and not worry about making equipment payments. It was that t-shirt business that jumpstarted my real estate journey and allowed me to bootstrap my way to real estate success.

Why I Chose Real Estate as My Wealth Opportunity

I always knew real estate would eventually become my path to wealth, which is why I decided to get my realtor's license at the age of 25. I hoped to make a million bucks selling real estate part-time at nights and weekends. Notice I said "hoped" rather than "planned." I quickly found out that being a successful realtor required far more time, work, and planning than I was prepared to invest. To make matters worse, I was not fond of desk duty or answering phones. Somehow, I was under the impression that once I became a realtor, clients would come knocking. I didn't realize that I would need to actively find clients through marketing, advertising, and even door-knocking.

I juggled working as a realtor on nights and weekends with my full-time job. My real estate career lasted a year, and I didn't make a single sale. However, it wasn't a total loss—come tax season, I was able to take advantage of legitimate business deductions. Real estate and business ownership remain two of the most favorable tax advantages in America today.

A few years after my stalled realtor career, I stumbled upon a late-night infomercial featuring a real estate guru named Carlton. He promised to teach people how to buy real estate for pennies on the dollar. I was hooked! I sent my hard-earned $235 to order the course and could hardly contain my excitement. I was going to buy real estate *on the cheap!* The course instructed me to search for property owners selling their homes by owner, then call them using his provided script and checklists. The goal was to find a motivated or desperate seller who would sell their property for 55 cents on the dollar or less. In addition, the seller would finance the property themselves, so I wouldn't need any money down.

That course introduced me to real estate investment training. It reignited the real estate flame in me. I quickly discovered, however, that much like being a licensed realtor, the Carlton course required me to pick up the phone and call people. The course scripts were designed to help lead me through the process, detailing what to say and when to say it. But for an introvert like me, calling strangers—especially to ask them to sell their home when—was daunting. I learned many real estate concepts, but let's just say that course was "very expensive tuition."

Even though my career as a realtor didn't pan out, I wasn't ready to abandon my dream of building wealth through real estate. After all, the wealthiest people in this country have achieved much of their success through real estate. Take Ray Kroc for instance, one of the founders of the McDonald's franchise. You may know McDonald's for its slogan, "Billions Served," but Kroc once asked his business school students a surprising question: "What business do you think I'm in?" Of course, everyone knew he was in the *hamburger* business. But he responded, "I'm not in the hamburger business. I'm in the real estate business." Today, McDonald's is one of the largest owners of real estate in the world. They control some of the most valuable intersections and street corners in the entire world.

My First Property – How I Bought a Duplex with T-Shirt Money

Earlier, I mentioned that screen printing has been one of my most successful ventures to date. Believe it or not, I bought my first property with the profits from selling t-shirts. Well, the truth is that I didn't literally swap t-shirts for the property as it sounds.

However, I used the proceeds from a t-shirt order for $500 as a down payment on an owner-financed duplex that I bought for $24,500. The owner literally became the bank, and I made monthly payments to them for the remainder of the $24,000. Little did I know, at the time, that I was buying the property on a land contract. A land contract is where you make payments to the seller and the seller holds the deed until the property is paid off in full. I will explain land contracts later in this book.

I initially found that deal when the owners advertised a duplex for sale in the local newspaper. The owners lived up north and inherited the property from their parents years earlier. Because they lived over 500 miles away, the family hired a local guy to manage the property. The property manager didn't do much more than collect the rent for as long as the property was in good repair. There was no preventive maintenance being done on the property and it showed. The place needed painting, repairs, and a general facelift, though one unit was still occupied.

It became clear that the property manager was tired of his job and barely maintaining the place. I think their original agreement with him was that he kept rent from one side and sent the owners rent from the other unit. According to the family, they had not received anything over the past few years and were still paying taxes on the property. I sensed frustration when talking with the owner. This place was causing them pain by constantly spending money and not receiving anything in return. To make matters worse, the property manager was a longtime family friend that they didn't want to fire or even offend. It was much easier for them to just get rid of the property.

They wanted the property gone but didn't want to entertain tire kickers either. So, they ran an ad in the local newspaper with just a just the fax number. Therefore, not many people pursued the property, even though they might have been curious. The very day I sent the fax, I received a call back with the name and number of the property manager.

I arranged a meeting and toured the duplex. One side was vacant, while the other was occupied, but interestingly, the vacant side was in better shape. Still, the property had its issues—sagging ceiling tiles, peeling paint, and deferred maintenance were obvious. The property manager gave me numerous excuses about the owners not wanting to spend money on repairs, etc. He said they told him to show the place so they could get it sold. Immediately after leaving, I called the owner's son back and asked, "Why are you selling such a nice property?" I learned to always ask that question, regardless of the condition of the property.

The owner's son immediately stated. "Mr. Adams hasn't sent any rent money in a long time. We're tired of paying taxes and collecting nothing."

My next question: "What would you need to get for the place?"

"We will take $24,500. If you pay $500 down, we will finance the rest."

That worked for me. We signed the closing papers at a McDonald's in the food court of a local mall in Raleigh, NC.

The terms were simple: $500 down and $200 a month for 48 months. Did you catch the interest rate? It was 0%. This was the first of several 0% interest deals to come. I officially bought this owner-financed deal, on a land contract where the seller holds the deed and doesn't transfer the title to the property until it's completely paid off. I still hold this property today, and it's been paid off for quite a few years now.

Chapter 2:

YOU'RE A GAZELLE – NOT A QUITTER!

Like many of you, I've faced countless opportunities to quit, to throw in the towel and justify it by saying, "Life isn't fair." The truth is life isn't fair—but it is consistent. If you do what successful people do, you will become successful. If you do what wealthy people do, you will become wealthy. Conversely, if you put nothing in, you get nothing out! It's one of those immutable laws in action. You can bet that at some point in life, you will be rewarded for your effort or punished for your lack of effort. Just be consistently persistent in working towards your goal.

I knew my grandfather and father weren't quitters, so giving up wasn't in my DNA. I witnessed my father's resilience and determination firsthand. I watched him go from bank to bank, trying to borrow money to build our home and move us off family property. Despite hearing "No" after "No," he did not give up. Instead, it fueled his resolve. He started building our house by hand with money from his paycheck every week. It took us 9 years of nights and weekends to complete that house, but when it was finished, he owned it free and clear.

As for me, if I were ever going to be a quitter, I could have easily given up on life when I was born on a cold day in the winter of 1958. I came into this world prematurely and weighed a mere

3 pounds and 3 ounces. But with all of that against me, I was determined to succeed regardless of the odds.

I learned many valuable life lessons through high school sports. I have never been very athletic, but I played football, basketball, wrestling, and track. Some of those sports seasons overlapped, so on those days, I went to both practices on the same day. Imagine leaving football practice and going directly to basketball practice or leaving basketball practice and going directly to track practice.

Sports reinforced my never-give-up attitude. There are many instances in sports when things don't go your way as a team and an individual. I recall when our track team was returning home from a track meet. Our school didn't have a track, so we had to run all our track meets at opposing schools. We were approximately 2 miles out of town when our bus just stopped and broke down along the road. We had to walk 2 miles back to school carrying our bags and track equipment all the way. There we were, the 30 of us walking along the highway with bags, vaulting poles, shot put discuss and other equipment.

Then there was the time the wrestling team bus stalled and cut off on the railroad tracks. School buses are required to stop at all railroad crossings. Our teen driver let off the clutch too quickly during takeoff and caused the bus to stall on the tracks. We could see the light from the slow-moving train coming toward us down the tracks. The driver quickly got the bus restarted and drove the tracks and headed home. Although we were never in real danger from the train, it was just enough to convince us to sit quietly the rest of the way home. Those were just some of the more memorable moments from sports that help develop "always finish what you start attitude."

Quitting never crossed my mind when I tried out for the high school track team. I was already a shot-putter, and I told the coach that I wanted to run the mile. There I stood, well over 200 pounds, lining up next to the lean, fast milers. When the coach fired the starting gun, I took off in a slow jog. The other runners left me far behind—so far, in fact, that the two-milers lapped me. Some of my teammates didn't hesitate to joke and rag me about being so slow.

My coach told me, probably out of pity, that he didn't have any track cleats in my size 12 shoe. He suggested that I stick to throwing shot put and discus, given my size, and said I'd have to earn a pair of running shoes. But I took it to heart. For the next year, I worked out and ran every single day. I wasn't just determined to outrun all the milers and two-milers. I had a new goal: to anchor the mile relay team, a position usually reserved for the fastest runner on the team.

The quarter-mile run (440 yards, which is now 400 meters) is an all-out sprint for one lap around the track. Just imagine running around your city block as fast as you can, when you reach halfway, someone gently lowers a dorm refrigerator onto your back. Then, for the last 100 yards, that refrigerator is suddenly filled with food, and the weight is doubled. I had a lot of work to do and 365 days to get it done. Every single day, rain or shine, I ran and worked out alone. No one knew the effort I was putting in—my teammates, never saw the hours I spent training by myself. But I was determined, focused, and had a clear plan for success.

You too will need that same level of determination, focus, and planning if you want to succeed in real estate investment. Just like my teammates, most people won't notice the hard work you put in behind the scenes; all they care about is whether you win or lose.

The next track season, one year later, I approached the coach and said, "Coach, I'm fast enough for the mile relay team. As a matter of fact, I want to anchor your relay team." He responded, "Line up and run with the quarter milers." He shot the starting gun, and I immediately left all the quarter milers and sprinters far behind. When the coach clocked me in the quarter mile, he looked at me in amazement and said, "Son, you've got gazelle speed! I'm ordering a pair of running shoes for you today! You are going to anchor my relay team."

At the time, I didn't know what a gazelle was, but I figured that a gazelle must be an animal that could run full speed for about three days. I was in that kind of shape just one year later after being mocked for being such a slow runner.

Those same teammates who teased me a year earlier had, unbeknownst to them, *inspired me to greatness*. You never know from whom or where your inspiration will come, so you must always be prepared. Develop a positive mindset with a plan to succeed, challenge yourself, be willing to operate outside your comfort zone, and be consistently persistent.

Chapter 3:

THE BOOTSTRAPPER IN YOU– IT'S OKAY TO START WITH NOTHING

Are you a bootstrapper at heart? Do you have a burning desire to succeed? Do you always dream of achieving more or creating something more? Even though you work a nine-to-five job, you are not absolutely thrilled with the work you do. Do you find yourself thinking of ways the job could be done better, faster, or more efficiently? You are good at what you do, but your gut keeps telling you that you still need your own. Are you constantly thinking about a side hustle or other opportunities away from work? Are you always dreaming about success opportunities that you share with others?

That's the entrepreneurial bug in you waiting to get out. The universe is telling you to get started now! As Dr. George Washington Carver said "Start where you are with what you have. Make something of it and never be satisfied."

A strong desire is critical to getting you jumpstarted as a bootstrapper. Desire will give you the motivation to get started, but the three main components needed to start and run any successful business, including real estate investment, are as follows:

1. Education or knowledge of the industry or profession.
2. The physical energy necessary to do the work.
3. The money or funding for the business.

It has been proven over time that you cannot start and run any successful business without all three. You don't have to personally possess all three, you just need to have access to all three.

Let's break them down.

First, **knowledge**–industry knowledge, practical knowledge, or understanding of the business. For instance, if you have 20 years of experience as a cook or a chef in a restaurant, it will be unreal to think that one day you would just go out and start an automotive repair shop with no experience in auto repair. I'm not suggesting that having expertise in one profession means you can't start a business in an entirely different field. What I'm saying is that you will need to acquire the education and experience from somewhere, whether by taking classes, working as an apprenticeship, volunteering, or some way. This book is one step toward your education in the real estate field.

Next, **time and energy** are crucial to running a business. Unless the business is truly passive, someone will need to run its day-to-day operations. You might find yourself in a situation where you have the energy but not the time. It could be a situation where you are working 12-hour shifts at your day job and can't break away to focus on the business during normal business hours. Or maybe you don't have the physical stamina for demanding work, like lifting heavy loads or working outdoors in tough conditions. No matter what, someone must bring the drive and energy to keep the business running smoothly.

Finally, **money or funding** is the key to every business, most businesses fail because of lack of it. So, how do we deal with the lack of funding? As bootstrappers, we tend to want to be all things to all people. But please understand that if you have the industry knowledge and energy, you can seek out funding from someone else. Funding can come from various sources: a home equity line of credit, a business line of credit, or even loans from family and friends. I will share numerous funding sources in the chapter called "Where to Find the Funding for Your Deals" later in this book.

Partnerships can be formed because one or more partners might have the complementary skills to operate a successful business. For instance, you chose my book because, as the title says, you don't have any money or good credit. But after reading my book, you will have:

1. education and knowledge of real estate investing and,
2. the time and energy to locate properties. All that's needed now is
3. money or funding, which could come from a friend, partner, lender, or even the seller.

The bootstrapper in me helped to overcome that lack of funding by gaining superior knowledge of creative dealmaking and having tremendous drive and energy. I was never going to let the lack of money stop me from succeeding in this business. I had to continually educate myself and stay motivated. My real estate education began in the '90s with books and tapes, which eventually evolved into CDs, thumb drives, and downloads. I vividly remember ordering books and tapes from gurus when they visited local real estate groups. They'd only bring a limited number of kits, if you didn't act fast, you had to wait for yours to arrive in the mail.

I was determined to succeed and get educated by any means necessary. I joined our local real estate investor group, North Carolina Real Estate Investors Association (NCREIA). Our mother organization is the National Real Estate Investor Association (National REIA), which consists of chapters nationwide. National REIA chapters are typically located in major metropolitan areas in each state. These groups provide excellent opportunities for real estate education and networking, usually meeting monthly. The meetings often feature national speakers or "gurus" who present on various aspects of real estate—and of course, they usually have something to sell, whether it's a course, coaching, or mentoring services.

If you're serious about real estate, I highly recommend finding and joining a local Real Estate Investor Association chapter. It's one of the best, most affordable ways to gain education and build connections in the industry. I rarely missed a local meeting when it started. I also visited other chapters when they had speakers I wanted to hear. I credit NCREIA for my formal real estate education. Even to this day, I recommend that all my students join the Real Estate Investor Association near them.

I also turned my car into a "university on wheels". My car was filled with CDs that I had listened to every day while driving. I didn't have a typical commute like most people, my "good" government job required me to drive four to five days a week. I spent a minimum of three hours behind the wheel daily, all the while listening to real estate and motivational CDs to get myself educated and to keep motivated. The technology progressed to audiobooks and ultimately to podcasts. I still listen to podcasts daily for education, inspiration, and entertainment.

UNDERSTANDING YOUR WHY-WHAT DRIVES YOU?

I've often heard, "Do what you love, and you will never work a day in your life." As Les Brown says, "People who are pursuing a dream have a certain glow about them." When you've found your calling, you will work tirelessly. I'm not suggesting that it's necessary to have an entrepreneurial mindset or spirit to go out and purchase just one house. But to be successful in real estate or any other business, you must understand what motivates you. It's called your WHY!

Your personal WHY could be as simple as wanting a house for yourself and your family. Maybe you're self-employed and can't show enough income to qualify for a traditional mortgage. Your WHY, could simply be your desire to get a house for your grandma to live out her last few years comfortably. Or it could be that you are a dreamer who wants to amass enough wealth for the next several generations. There could be any number of reasons why you choose to get involved in real estate.

When I started in real estate, I had a "good" government job with decent pay and a respectable retirement plan. But I knew deep down that I wanted to create generational wealth, and nobody's job was going to do that for me. I didn't want my children, grandchildren, and great-grandchildren to have the same struggles that I had to endure. I wanted to leave them with enough resources to be able to choose education and careers based on their interests and their desires. I don't want them to get an education based on just getting a good paying job.

When I think about my WHY, I'm reminded of a friend of mine, a schoolmate from college. Here is a quick story about my friend Lee Stephenson of Midlothian VA. Lee shared with me his remarkable journey of pursuing his college degree. He had originally enrolled in college right out of high school. During that first year of school, he got married and started a family and left school for financial reasons. He joined the Army and served three years of active duty. When he got out of the Army he went back home and got a job locally. Lee had a burning desire to continue his education. But he knew with a wife and two children to support, he couldn't quit his job and go back to school full-time.

Through the encouragement of several of his high school teachers, he re-enrolled at Elizabeth City State University, to continue his education. I saw Lee on campus daily and interacted with him in a few classes. I knew there was something different about Lee and his college experience, but I couldn't quite put my finger on it. I later found out; while attending school, he worked a full-time job at a shipyard about 45 miles away while carrying a full course load as a student. In addition to his job and course load, he commuted up to 210 miles roundtrip daily for 3 years from his hometown of Murfreesboro, NC to Elizabeth City State University in Elizabeth City, NC.

I think Lee's strong desire to complete his education was a model of commitment and perseverance. He felt that his daily commute was a small price to pay for an opportunity to improve his life and the life of his family. He went on to graduate and spent over 30 years teaching and working with disadvantaged youth.

QUIT THE NEGATIVE SELF-TALK

What's holding you back from getting started in real estate today? After all, it doesn't require any money, nor does it require good credit. Is it that internal self-talk that keeps telling you that you can't do this, you can't do that. It's saying you're not old enough, you're not rich enough, you're not this and you're not that. That self-talk will also begin to make excuses like, that person became successful because they were born into money, they knew the right people. Get rid of that negative self-talk!

Over the years, I've listened to all the top real estate gurus in the country, and without fail, they all say, "If I can do this business, anyone can." They're right—anyone *can* learn real estate concepts and become an investor. But here's the stark truth: only about 3% of the people who buy these courses ever take action and do a deal.

I've attended real estate conferences where people rushed to the back of the room to purchase the books tapes and just think only three people out of every hundred will ever use the course to improve their lives. Yes, the other 97% can do it, but what's holding them back from ever attempting to reach for their dreams and desires? They are all pumped and excited when they swipe that credit card, but somewhere between the swipe and the time they get home, something changes. What has changed?

The conference speaker had a rag-to-riches story that was so compelling that it would almost bring tears to your eyes. The energy in the room is contagious—everyone's pumped, their mindset full of "I can do it" confidence. You're so motivated that you crack open the course materials and listen to the CDs on your drive home, thinking, *This is it! I'm going to be successful in real estate! I'll start on Monday, launch a marketing plan, and the deals will roll in.* Just like the guru said, you'll follow the course step by step and become rich and successful, just like them.

Then when you get home, reality begins to set in, life happens. You share your excitement and your information with your spouse or partner. He/she doesn't seem to be nearly as excited about the possibilities as you are. That's understandable because they didn't see and hear how Mr. Guru overcame all those life challenges and now, he's wealthy beyond his dreams because of real estate. Regardless, I am still pumped and motivated enough for both of us. I can make it happen, and they will get on board once they see me have some success.

The next day at work, you're still glowing with motivation. When your coworkers ask what you did over the weekend, you can't wait to tell them about the Get Rich Quick Real Estate Seminar that you attended over the weekend. You get even more excited talking about how rich you are going to be and how you will soon be quitting this job to do real estate full-time. You start talking to coworkers in industry jargon using terms like Mortgage Wraps, Subject -to, Land Trusts, Options, and other real estate terms. Most of them will casually end the conversation and quietly move on, especially after you tell them that the Guru said that you can invest in real estate with no money and bad credit.

Please don't become discouraged. Family, friends, and co-workers will often try to protect you from failure and disappointment. They mean well—they want you to be happy. But most people live their entire lives in their comfort zone. They play it safe, avoiding any risks, even calculated ones. They want steady paychecks and the security or something familiar. While their intentions are honorable, they're not the ones who will push you toward success in real estate—or anything else.

You shouldn't fault them for wanting a day job that has a consistent paycheck every week or every other week. You too need a paycheck every other week to pay bills and other financial obligations. Maybe you should stand on the nearest mountain and yell out to all those folks, "I am not going to quit my day job cold turkey to get into the real estate business! I'm going to work that day job just like you. But I swear to you that I will spend every waking moment away from work pursuing my real estate investment dreams. I am prepared to use every ounce of drive and determination that I have, to make real estate work for me.

I once came across this quote: "Change the people you are around or change the people you are around." I can't remember exactly which guru said it, but I wish I did so I could give them proper credit. Regardless, it stuck with me, and it's something I recommend you reflect on deeply.

I suggest that you take an honest look at the people around you. Ask yourself: Does this person bring positive energy or negative energy into my life? This will be difficult because some will be family and close friends that you have known for years. For those that bring positive energy, continue to share successes, milestones, and bits of knowledge with them and slowly bring them along with you on your journey to success. I should not have to tell you how to handle those with negative energy.

When I first started in real estate, I was cautious about how I discussed real estate with my circle of friends and acquaintances.

Instead of proclaiming, "I'm going to be rich from real estate," I would casually bring up the topic and gauge their reactions. Were they curious? Did they ask questions? Or were they skeptical, maybe even dismissive? Were they genuinely happy for me, or did they play devil's advocate? These conversations helped me decide how close I wanted each person to remain within my inner circle.

Further, being the analytical introvert that I am, I was literally listening to everything they said and didn't say. I watched their body language, listened to subtle cues, and took everything into account.

When I went back and analyzed conversations that I had been having with my circle I found that most of the conversations involved television, sports, and politics. I must admit that there was a phase in my life when I watched sports, primarily football, like a junkie. In 1996, I made a conscious decision to stop watching football on television and decided to use those 7 hours on Sunday afternoons to educate myself and work on my business. My network and my net worth grew in direct proportion to the time that I invested in my real estate education. I was determined to succeed!

Along the way, I also met other like-minded investors at our local real estate investor meetings. I have a circle of friends that I met at the local REIA that I still communicate and network with to this day. We all have varying skill sets and specialties as it relates to real estate investing. It's good to have someone bounce ideas off from time to time. Join your local real estate investor group and it will help you "change your friends or change your friends."

Chapter 4:

HOW TO MAKE MONEY WITH NO MONEY – THE SECRETS

The main ways to make money in real estate is by being a birddog (property scout), wholesaling, leasing and subleasing, rehabbing, or buying and holding as rentals. There are many other ways to make money in real estate, such as buying notes, lending money, etc. But for the purposes of this book, we will focus primarily on bird-dogging, wholesaling and leasing as the primary ways to get started with little or no money.

We will also discuss acquisition techniques called buying on land contract and buying *Subject-to Existing Financing.*

I will take some time to explain the concepts of bird-dogging and wholesaling, as these terms may be unfamiliar to you. Rehabbing and buying and holding are self-explanatory, so I won't cover them in this chapter, although I will touch on those topics later in the book.

The term "bird-dog" comes from the actions of a bird dog when used for hunting birds. Just imagine for a minute that you are watching a hunter and his bird dog. The bird dog's role is to identify the location of the bird's nesting area. The dog will then stop completely still and point out the location of the birds for the hunter.

Similarly, a real estate birddog or property scout provides referrals. Their main responsibility is to identify properties where the owners are motivated to sell. This could include vacant or abandoned properties, homes in need of repair, or owners facing financial distress. Investors are willing to pay for leads on these properties, even if you can only provide the address. Ideally, it's helpful to also include the owner's name, contact information, and their reason for selling. The more information you can gather, the better, but investors will still pay you even if you only provide an address.

Bird-dogging is easy, doesn't require any money, and doesn't require much of a time commitment either. For instance, a friend tells you that they are having to move because the house they are renting is about to be foreclosed. You can pick up the phone and call an investor and give the investor the property address, the owner's name, and phone number. That investor will pay you a minimum of $1,000 for that lead if they close the deal. Just think, you can make a quick $1,000 or more just for picking up the phone and alerting an investor to an existing opportunity.

Some folks bird-dog for a living, and they probably make a pretty good side hustle. But I would think that making $1,000 for a lead is more of a hustle rather than a long-term business strategy. If you are a student, homemaker, or someone with no capital, bird-dogging can be a great way to get started while learning about wholesaling. You can use the proceeds from your first few deals to cover marketing costs and launch your wholesaling business.

BIRD-DOGGING: HOW I DID A QUICK $1,500.00 BIRDDOG DEAL

In my investing career, I have only bird-dogged one deal. I was marketing to probate attorneys within about a hundred-fifty mile radius of my city. I had sent an attorney a couple of letters about buying other probate properties. That attorney kept my contact information on file and when she ran across another property that met my criteria, she called me.

Although I had no intention of buying and rehabbing a property in her area, I decided to contact a local I Buy Houses franchisee and sold the lead to them for $1,500. They, the rehabber, negotiated the deal, closed on it, and I received a nice check for $1,500. All I had done was make a phone call and refer a property that I'd never seen, even to this day. That particular property lead only cost me the price of a postage stamp, which I think was less than .60 cents back then. Property scouting or bird-dogging is the quickest way to get started on the cheap. Again, you can use the proceeds from bird-dogging to increase your marketing budget, to pay for additional education, and save up funds to start wholesaling.

You can work as a birddog or property scout for someone else or you can have property scouts working for you. You could offer a flat dollar amount to anyone who brings you a property that you end up buying. Some professions to target would be:

- Postal workers
- Cable company workers
- Garbage collectors

- Dumpster rental companies
- Moving and storage like U-Haul
- Electric utility workers
- Fire Department
- Shipping companies, UPS, Fed Ex, etc.

You can pay them a flat fee for each lead or offer to pay them if or when the lead closes. You could then sell that lead to a rehabber or another investor or get the property under contract and flip the contract. More on flipping contracts later under Wholesaling.

Chapter 5:

I MAKE MONEY WHOLESALING PROPERTIES

Wholesaling has served me well over the years in this business, allowing me to accumulate enough cash to buy and hold rental properties. Some people refer to this practice as flipping properties, often lumping wholesalers and rehabbers into one broad category and calling both "flippers." However, most wholesalers don't actually close on the properties that they profit from. In fact, some states now have regulations requiring wholesalers to close on a property before reselling it to a rehabber or landlord.

Typically, a wholesaler will identify a property and get the property under contract, with a *Purchase and Sale Agreement*. The wholesaler will then find a cash buyer and sell the contract for a fee. Keep in mind that the wholesaler is only selling the contract and not the property.

The wholesaler (Assignor) assigns his or her purchase rights to the end buyer Assignee, giving the end buyer the right to step in and close on the property. The end buyer is now the new owner of the property, and the wholesaler has received a fee either before closing or at closing. In many cases wholesalers can earn assignment fees of $5,000.00 – $15,000 or more depending on the price that the wholesaler and the end buyer agree on.

Please note that wholesaling laws are being challenged and changed state-by-state. Your state laws might not allow the end buyer (your assignee) on a wholesale deal to use their funds to close. Those states require that the wholesaler that put the property under contract must first close on the property and then in a separate transaction sell the property to the end buyer at a separate closing.

One solution is for you, the wholesaler, to borrow funds from a transactional lender to close the deal and assign it on the same day. For example, you could close the deal with the seller at 9:00 AM, then hold a second closing with the end buyer (assignee) at 10:00 AM. This allows you (the assignor) to repay the transactional loan within just a few hours. Transactional lenders typically charge a small percentage of the loan amount as interest for using their funds temporarily. However, that small interest payment is often well worth it to close the deal and put money in your pocket.

HOW TO DETERMINE YOUR WHOLESALE FEE

You're probably wondering how to determine a wholesale fee. You might also be wondering what stops a person from selling their contract for an inflated price, say, for $50,000 over their price from the seller? First, the property must be cheap enough for the rehabber or landlord to make money on the deal after repairing it. There is a standard formula called the wholesaling formula. Here's how we arrive at the figures for a wholesale deal. We start with the *After Repair Value,* (ARV) times 70%, then minus the repairs that are needed, and that number will give you your *Maximum Allowable Offer* (MAO) or *Purchase Price* (PP), which is the most we can pay for the property. Once we have determined our MAO, we then subtract out our wholesale fee. The number that we get after subtracting our wholesale fee is the maximum price we can pay for the property. Here is the Wholesaling Formula:

ARV x 70% – Repairs – Wholesale Fee = Purchase Price (PP)

Let's break that down:

- **ARV** = After Repair Value (what the property will be worth after renovations)
- **70% Rule** = Investors typically want to buy at 70% of ARV to leave room for profit
- **Repairs** = Estimated cost to get the property into shape
- **Wholesale Fee** = What you want to make on the deal
- **PP** = The maximum price you can pay the seller

Example Breakdown

Let's plug in some real numbers:

- **ARV**: $200,000
- **70% of ARV**: $200,000 x 0.7 = **$140,000 (MAO)**
- **Repairs**: $40,000
- **Wholesale Fee**: $10,000

Now apply the formula:

$140,000 – $40,000 – $10,000 = $90,000 (Purchase Price to seller)

So, if you want to make a $10,000 wholesale fee and keep your investor happy, you can't offer the seller more than $90,000. This structure helps you work backward from what your buyer will pay, ensuring everyone wins—the seller, the end buyer, and you.

Novice investors would look at this deal in a negative manner and will allow the negative mindset to creep in. They would somehow convince themselves that "this person has a house that can be worth $200,000 fixed up. They will never sell that house to me for $90,000. There is no way that anyone would accept that little bit of money for their $200,000 house."

The novice investor will talk themselves out of making the offer because they feel that their offer looks too low. Going forward, always make the offer after running the numbers regardless of how you feel about the numbers. Let the property owner tell you no. But at least make the offer. Also, I will pass on a little advice that this Bootstrapper learned from the School of Hard Knocks. If you are not downright embarrassed of your offer, then your offer is too high.

Keep in mind that wholesale deals are made every day because folks have varying degrees of motivation in society. Perhaps someone has just accepted a new job in another part of the country and must relocate within 2 weeks. Another person could be facing eminent legal problems and need access to quick cash. There will always be motivated sellers in society and if you are not willing to help them with their problem then the next investor will.

Get over your fear of making offers and most importantly, get over your fear of making lowball offers. If you make an offer that is too high and they accept it, then you won't be able to assign your contract to the end buyer. You will just have to go back to the seller and negotiate a lower price. That will be one awkward conversation with the seller. Ask me how I know!

A lot of folks started out in the real estate investment business as wholesalers due to the low barrier to entry. Your primary overhead will typically be marketing costs and the *Earnest Money Deposit* (EMD). The earnest money deposit required when securing a property under contract can be as low as $10 to $100, depending on the seller's agreement.

Some of the advantages of wholesaling are that again, it doesn't cost much to get started and you can learn while you're earning money. In other words, you can make money while you are working on other skills like understanding, rehabbing, understanding repair costs, and all those kinds of things. Wholesaling also allows you to build up cash to be used for rehabbing or to buying and holding rentals in the future.

When I was wholesaling regularly, I cherry-picked the properties and kept the better deals for myself to hold as rentals. I still hold those rentals today and they have created wealth for me over time.

Chapter 6:

THE 12 STEPS TO A WHOLESALE DEAL

In the previous section, I introduced the concept of wholesaling. Now, we will walk step-by-step through the wholesaling process using the attached 12 Steps. We will end the chapter with a fictitious wholesaling scenario that I created. I intentionally added a few wrinkles to this scenario so that I could "drop some nuggets" so to speak. For novice investors, those nuggets will improve your learning curve exponentially. Even seasoned investors will learn a bit here to sharpen their skills.

The 12 Steps to A Wholesale Deal

STEP 1: Market to advertise for distressed sellers – mailings, cold calls, internet, etc.

STEP 2: Find a vacant property – overgrown grass weeds, broken windows, etc.

STEP 3: Locate the property owner – talk to neighbors, county tax office, obituary, skip trace.

STEP 4: Talk to the owner – find motivation, build rapport, and access the property.

STEP 5: Inspect the property – Walk the property with a contractor to estimate repairs.

STEP 6: Determine the Maximum Allowable Offer (MAO) – run comparable sales (Comps).

STEP 7: Negotiate with the seller – find their price, reinforce their motivation, and push for terms.

STEP 8: Sign contract with the seller – give Earnest Money Deposit (EMD), as little as $100.

STEP 9: Get the signed contract to an attorney or title company – they start a title search.

STEP 10: Find end buyer (rehabber or landlord) – your local REIA, other marketing.

STEP 11: Assign the contract to end buyer – Contract Assignment Agreement.

STEP 12: Closing – follow the process to closing at the title company or attorney.

A Wholesale Scenario

Step 1: Marketing

I always initiate contact through mailings, never opting for cold calls, texts, or emails. When someone calls me in response to my mailing, they give me implied consent to return the call or contact them again in the future. Their decision to call me indicates that they are engaging with me at their convenience, making them more likely to be receptive, even if they aren't ready to sell at that time. In some cases, the owner may have already set a selling price.

If they don't call me after several postcards or letters, I will sometimes skip trace to find their phone number and call them directly. Please keep in mind that I don't do cold calling at all as part of my business model. When I call the property owner, I introduce myself and say, "I'm calling to follow up on the mailings that I sent you regarding the property located at 123 Main Street, is now a good time to talk?"

Step 2: Find a Vacant Property – What Properties I Look For

Recently, while driving through my neighborhood, I spotted a vacant, rundown house that hadn't been lived in for years. I recall there used to be an older couple living there, but I'm uncertain whether they have passed away or moved in with family. My objective is to locate the owner of this dilapidated house, secure it under contract, and then flip that contract to a rehabber or landlord for a nice profit.

I'm looking for signs of a vacant abandoned property. The most obvious is overgrown grass and bushes, the mailbox is torn off or stuffed with mail and old newspapers and sales flyers lying in the driveway. There are no curtains or window dressings and numerous other small telltale signs that indicate that no one is living in this property. The clogged gutters are beginning to sag, and the windows look like they haven't been washed in years.

It appears on the outside to be the typical vacant property with overgrown bushes and trees growing all around the house.

However, someone is keeping the grass cut frequently enough to satisfy the city and code enforcement.

There are plenty of houses out here that are sitting and decaying as we speak, just remember "there is a buyer for every house." There are rehab buyers who specialize in major gut jobs that don't care about structural or foundation issues. Other buyers specialize in fire damaged and burned-out properties and of course, some builders like to buy teardowns and rebuild on infill lots. So don't let the condition of a property scare you away, the uglier, the better when it comes to making money on abandoned properties.

Step 3: Locate The Owner

I always talk to as many neighbors as possible. I try to get as much information about the property as I can possibly get from each neighbor. There is usually a story about the house and almost always someone nearby who keeps an eye on the property whether voluntarily or by request of the owner. Also, neighbors have a vested interest in maintaining the appearance of their neighborhood. They are usually delighted to find out that someone wants to fix up an abandoned property. Removing that old eyesore would improve the overall appearance of the neighborhood and add value to their individual homes also. You should find most neighbors to be very cooperative in providing information where possible.

Unfortunately, there can be some instances where the neighbors really don't know who owns the property, but don't let this discourage you. There are numerous free sources available to find owners, as well as several paid sources. I will start with the quickest free source, which is the county Tax Office. You can call the county tax office and give them the property address and ask them to whom and where the tax bill is being sent. They will provide the responsible party's name as well as their mailing address. You can also search for this same information online in most counties in this country.

Now, what if the tax bill is still being sent to the vacant property address? That just means that we still have a little more detective work to do. The good thing is that we now have the name of the owner or responsible party; the next step is to locate that individual. I start by checking online obituaries to see if the responsible party, or any variation of their name, appears, to determine if they are still living.

Additionally, I will search social media sites and online incarceration records also to see if I can find them without spending any money at all. If neither of those pan out then I would pay for an online skip trace service to provide me with their address, phone number, email, and social media contact information. If they can't be located through the skip tracing service then I would consider hiring a bail bondsman or detective to locate them, especially if it is a property where I stand to make a lot of cash.

Step 4: Talk to The Owner

I have a few simple goals for that initial call. I am trying to find out: (1) the owner's level of motivation (2) get access to view the property (3) build a rapport.

Vacant and abandoned property owners have varying levels of motivation. Just because a property is vacant doesn't mean the owner is eager to sell. I have sent over 200,000 mailings to vacant properties over the years, and some of those have remained vacant for over 20 years. Many owners are content to pay the taxes and allow their property to sit idle indefinitely. As an investor, your task is to remind them of the costs and liabilities associated with owning a vacant property, offering to relieve them of that burden by purchasing their problematic asset.

Step 5: Inspect The Property

Once the owner grants me access, I will line up as many general contractors, tradespeople, and potential buyers as I possibly can so that they can walk the property with me. Sometimes the owner will give me the key and allow me to access the property as often as I wish to do my inspection. There are other times when the owner will only allow access to the property for a few hours, and they want to be present or have their representative during that short time. As a practice, if an owner gives me the access key, I will make sure to inform them each time before I go in and after I leave. This serves two purposes: (A) it protects me in case the property is left open, unsecured, or further damaged during my access, and (B) it creates another opportunity for communication, which helps to build rapport.

Step 6: Build Rapport

We all know that people do business with folks they know and like. You must build rapport and trust with someone if they are going to sell you, their property. Business books tell us that we must have at least 7 touches to establish rapport with someone. I generally try to find out how they like to communicate best (phone, text, in person, etc.) and make sure that I use their favorite method of communication as much as possible. As I mentioned earlier, I let them know each time I access their property with the key, this gives me more opportunities to communicate and increases the number of touches.

I honestly want to know what the owners plan to do with the money. So, once I begin to build a rapport with them, I will ask them point-blank "What are you going to do with the money?" Why is that important to me? It's important to me because of *Terms*. This might shock you, but most people don't need money. They need the things that money can buy for them. Some people don't want or need a big chunk of money at one time because of their silent partner, the IRS. They are more comfortable taking payments and paying a smaller proportion of their income in taxes and paying taxes only as they become due.

I walk through the property with my general contractor and have them come up with a repair estimate. When I started wholesaling, I read somewhere that you will need to look at 200 houses before you become good at estimating repairs. It sounded like a large number at the time, but I think I had looked at over 200 before I became good at it.

When starting, you probably won't be able to estimate repairs accurately either unless you happen to work in the trades. I recommend finding a friendly local general contractor, handyman, or skilled tradesperson and ask them to accompany you on the first few deals. Take notes, ask questions, and learn as much about estimating repairs as you can and eventually you will learn to estimate repairs accurately by yourself. Also, don't forget to compensate the general contractor and others for their time. If not, they probably won't pick up the phone the next time you call.

Step 6: Determine the Property Value and Your Maximum Allowable Offer

I determine my maximum allowable offer (MAO) by using comparable sales to determine what the property can be sold for fixed up. Here is the formula again:

MAO = ARV x .70 – Repair Costs.

Step 7: Negotiate With the Seller

My next step is to call the seller back and negotiate the offer. I could write a couple of entire books on the topic of negotiation, which is said to be the most lucrative and highest-paid profession in the world. But I will confine this chapter to three basic techniques that almost anyone can learn to utilize with relative ease after a little practice.

My objective in negotiating with the seller is to come up with a price and terms that work for both of us. I never want to hammer a seller into submission. I have been in this business for over 20 years and plan to continue indefinitely. I want the seller to feel just as good about the deal as I did. We want to make it a win-win for both of us.

My 3 Favorite Negotiating Techniques to Find Their Asking Price

When I am trying to find out their asking price – I begin by addressing them directly: "Mr./Ms. [Last Name], what would you need to make this deal happen?" Then, I pause and remain silent. Most people find silence uncomfortable and will start talking, often negotiating against themselves in the process.

You've probably heard the saying "The first one to mention price is the loser." I will ask them their price several times but pose the question in several different ways to get their asking price. If they still don't mention their price, I will look at them and smile and say, "I'm guessing that the property is worth more than one dollar, but I know it's not worth 1 million dollars, so we just have to find that number somewhere in between". This usually provokes a laugh, which helps relax the atmosphere and allows us to move forward with the negotiation.

I also make it a point to wince when the seller mentions their asking price. Even if on the phone, when they mention price, you just act as if you had the wind knocked out of you. Most sellers will view this as an indication that their asking price is too high and sometimes start negotiating against themselves. Most sellers won't have a method for determining their sales price, so I will just ask "How did you arrive at that price?"

I have received all kinds of answers: "That's the tax value; that's the amount I need to pay off the mortgage and buy a new vehicle; that's what it appraised for three years ago; that's what my neighbor's newly remodeled HGTV house sold for." Sellers often rely on what I call the SWAG Method (Strategic Wild Ass Guess) when setting their prices. As an informed investor, it's your job to establish a price that can be supported by comparable sales. One word of caution: if a seller asks you how much their house is worth, don't get drawn into that trap. My response is, "Ms. Seller, I can't tell you how much your property is worth; I can only tell you how much we can afford to pay for it."

The third and final negotiating technique that I promised you is called "mirroring and pacing" Mirroring is simply mimicking the seller's posture, for instance, if they cross their arms, you cross your arms, etc. Pacing is to talk and respond at the same pace as the seller. For instance, I talk slowly, and I tend to be very deliberate at times. However, if the seller talks fast then I must speed up my speaking pace to align with theirs.

Step 8: Sign The Purchase and Sale Agreement

Once we agree on a price, I will have the seller sign our Purchase and Sale Agreement (PSA). I don't use the State Licensed Realtor's Sales Contract, as a matter of fact, I don't even mention the word "contract" and I say "agreement" instead. When some people hear the word "contract," they assume it was created by a lawyer and that they need their own lawyer to review it before signing. I'm not trying to hide anything or be dishonest with any seller, but a lawyer can and will kill your deal if you let them. Therefore, I read the Purchase and Sale Agreement to them word for word and explained each line and paragraph. I also tell them that if there is absolutely anything in the agreement that they don't agree with, then just draw a line through it and we both will initial.

Also, for a contract to be valid there must be some "consideration" which typically is money that is held as the *Earnest Money Deposit* (EMD). The amount of the EMD is whatever you and the seller agree to and should be held by the closing attorney or title company. Please don't write an EMD check directly to the seller and ask them to hold the check. Sometimes the seller will cash the check and declare it their windfall.

Ask me how I know... yes, it happened to me once. I had a seller who had a for sale by owner (FSBO) sign out front, but he was not very motivated to sell. I negotiated him down to a great lowball price and wrote him a small EMD check to seal the deal. He got cold feet, cashed my check, and then told me that he was no longer interested in selling. The check that he cashed was for $100.00, but it would have cost me $126.00 to take them to small claims court. I just moved on to the next opportunity and considered that $100.00 as cheap tuition for that education.

Step 9: Get Signed Contract to Attorney or Title Company

Step 10: Find End Buyer (Assignee)

If I did not already have a cash buyer lined up, I would immediately begin to market the property online, at local investor meetings, through bandit signs, flyers, or any number of ways to find a cash buyer. **NOTE: Never attempt to market a property until you have it under contract.**

Step 11: Assignment Contract with End Buyer

Once we agreed on the price, terms, and closing date. I will contact my (Assignee) cash buyer who has already walked the property with me, the (Assignor) and we will sign a *Contract Assignment Agreement* allowing them to step into my position as the buyer and close on the property. The assignment agreement will list my assignment fee amount, and their EMD amount and show whether I get paid immediately or at closing.

The time window between signing the P&SA and closing is critical and could require a lot of behind-the-scenes communication on your part. The first task will be to locate a wholesale-friendly attorney or title company in the area. I try to get the signed P&SA over to the attorney as soon as possible so they can start the title search as soon as possible. We don't want anything to delay the closing and allow any party the opportunity to come up with excuses not to close this deal. It's a delicate balancing act with having to keep the seller informed of the progress and reassured that the closing will be done on the date as agreed.

The Assignee might have questions that only the seller can answer and it's part of my responsibility to get the answers and respond quickly. This can be a busy time for me but that's why we get paid as investors. Some of us earn those wholesale fees that we get paid.

Step 12: Closing Day

I find out in advance from the seller if they want to attend the closing in person or have the closing done electronically or by overnight mail. Most of the sellers I dealt with in the past were older or lived out of town. I try to make the closing as convenient for them as possible because I want the transaction to be seamless to reduce the likelihood of indecision. I always show up at the closings and pick up my big check.

Chapter 7:

CONTROL WITHOUT OWNERSHIP – MAKE MONEY LEASING AND SUBLEASING

Thus far, we've covered a couple of quick and simple ways to get started making money in real estate when you have little or no money. Those two ways were bird dogging and wholesaling. A logical next step in your real estate investing journey is leasing and subleasing. Leasing doesn't require much money, usually just a small deposit and funds to get the property in rental condition. Just as you have learned to identify vacant properties to wholesale, you could easily cherry-pick some of the better properties to lease and sublease if the numbers work.

This chapter will break down leasing into three distinct areas:

- **Leasing and subleasing long-term** at a higher and better use.
- **Rental Arbitrage** – leasing and subleasing short-term rentals (STR) and mid-term rentals (MTR). I like to differentiate between long-term subleasing at a higher and better use versus short term rentals.
- **Buying on lease option,** where you position yourself to ultimately own the property. We will cover the required

paperwork and the things you should consider and include in your option paperwork. I will even use my first lease option deal as a case study.

Imagine this, you legally collect rent checks every month — but you don't even own the property! This isn't about being a property manager (which often requires a broker's license). Instead, it's about **leasing a property from a landlord and then renting it out to others at a higher rate** — pocketing the difference. Here are just some of the advantages of leasing:

- **Cheap entry:** Control a property for a few hundred dollars or less
- **No attorney, no closing, no title company needed** — simple paperwork
- **Rent it out and profit without owning**
- **Test drive before buying**
- **Add value to tired or problem properties** by finding new rental uses

You can take those tired properties and find a higher and better use for them.

Leasing and subleasing isn't something new, and it's probably been going on since the beginning of time. The process is pretty straightforward, but you will need to know and understand the rental market in your area. You can start out by identifying a vacant property or a tired landlord. You then have a conversation with the owner to understand their pain points to determine their motivation. The conversation could go something like this: "I would like to rent this property from you as is, and I am willing to fix it up to livable condition on my dime. I will take care of all minor repairs going forward, and I will send you a monthly rent check of $500 every month guaranteed. Of course, I'm going to sublease it and make money on the spread. You will not have to deal with tenants, toilets and trash and you will be able to spend more time doing what you like to do. Is that something you would consider? To make this arrangement mutually beneficial, I'll need a lease term of at least 3 to 5 years."

Even if you are not a total skeptic, you might ask yourself, *why would a person lease their property to me knowing that I am going to rent it out for a higher rate? Why don't they just rent it out themselves, avoid me as the middleman, and make more money for themselves?*

There will always be someone with a property that they either can't sell or won't sell for various reasons. There will also be landlords or homeowners with vacant properties and are unable to find qualified renters. Your role is to identify existing landlords or homeowners and talk with them about how advantageous it would be for them to lease their property to you, rather than someone else.

Here are just a few of the reasons that someone might lease their property to you as an investor and allow you to sublease it.

- **Tired of managing tenants** — toilets, trash, calls, headaches

- **Vacant property hard to rent** due to location, condition, size, or neighborhood decline
- **Mortgage greater than the property value** — can't sell without loss or tax pain
- Want **guaranteed monthly rent** without the management hassle
- Homeowners **unable to sell quickly or profitably**
- Owners **relocating** or needing quick cash flow

A homeowner might be open to leasing their property to you because they are unable to sell it quickly and for a profit. They might just flat out owe more on the mortgage than the property is worth, which means that they would have to bring a check to closing just to get it sold. I've had a bit of success with leasing from folks who are behind on their mortgage or folks who are relocating for their jobs, when the property is not fixed up to sell quickly. Another likely candidate is someone with a property that needs major repairs that they can't afford to make.

Again, it is very important that you know and understand the rental market in your area. Before signing any contract, you want to be certain that you will be able to lease that property at a higher and better rate, enabling you to make a monthly profit., higher rate and be able to make a monthly profit. Also, consider all expenses, and don't forget insurance and marketing.

We get paid in this business by solving other people's problems. You become the hero by offering landlords peace of mind and a steady income — while you take on the management and rental tasks.

I've outlined a few ways where landlords might have a perceived problem. Here are just a few scenarios that you may encounter, along with solutions.

PROBLEM: Big, Obsolete House with Too Many Bedrooms

Some older homes were built with four, five, or even six bedrooms—great in the 1950s, but not as marketable today. These houses sit vacant because traditional renters aren't interested.

SOLUTION:

- Convert the home into a **boarding house**, renting by the room.
- Lease the entire property to an **agency or nonprofit** as a **group home**, **transitional housing**, or **sober living facility**.

This increases income potential and fills a housing need in your community.

PROBLEM: Small 1-Bedroom House

Tiny houses are tough to rent to families or traditional tenants. They often get passed over because of their size alone.

SOLUTION:

- Market to **truck drivers**, **traveling nurses**, or others whose jobs keep them away from home for long stretches.
- **Furnish** the house and reposition it as a **tiny home** or **short-term cottage rental**.

The goal is to match the space to a niche audience who values low maintenance and simplicity.

PROBLEM: Property in a Noisy Industrial Area

Properties near factories, highways, or train tracks can be difficult to fill with traditional tenants due to noise and traffic.

SOLUTION:

- Rent the home by the **room** to individuals who value low cost over location.
- Lease the **yard or driveway space** to **contractors**, **delivery companies**, or **small fleets** for **parking and storage**.

Industrial doesn't always mean undesirable; it just calls for a different kind of tenant.

PROBLEM: Small Commercial Garage or Storefront

A tiny storefront or standalone garage might be too small for a single tenant to justify leasing the full space.

SOLUTION:

- **Subdivide** the space with temporary walls to create **individual stalls** for mechanics, hobbyists, or artists.
- Use the space for **pop-up retail**—monthly rentals for vendors, boutiques, or weekend markets.

This approach creates multiple income streams from a single underutilized property.

RENTAL ARBITRAGE – THE SHARING ECONOMY BOOM

The shared housing industry has become so lucrative that savvy investors can lease properties from others at or above market rates and then sublease them to others at much higher rates for short-term stays. The industry refers to this as Rental Arbitrage. Short-term rentals (STR) usually offer nightly stays up to 30 days. The midterm rentals (MTR) offer stays of 30 days and longer, up to 1 year. The short-term rental (includes and MTR) business is a $135-billion-dollar industry worldwide. There was over $19 billion spent on short-term rental here in the U. S. alone in 2024.

Technology has allowed this industry to explode over the last decade. There are now phone apps that allow hosts and guests to communicate in real time. A guest can book a stay in someone's home anywhere in the world using an app on their phone. They can book a stay, pay for the stay and receive a passcode to digitally unlock and lock the doors. They can end their stay and check out of the unit without any human contact.

You can begin making money in the STR industry without spending a lot upfront. I first got involved in the MTR business in 2018, when I purchased a small apartment complex that included a couple of one-bedroom units located above the parking garages. I spent a few thousand dollars furnishing those units including beds, linens silverware, just like a typical extended stay hotel.

If you're renting STR to families and vacationers, your furnishings will need to be higher end to meet their expectations.

Typically, vacationers are looking to stay in a place that's nicer than their own homes, with more amenities. Vacationers can be a little more persnickety than business travelers.

I focused on renting to healthcare professionals and other travel professionals in town for work. I know my own temperament, tolerance, and limitations. I chose MTR primarily because I didn't want to deal with tourists, families, and vacationers. Also, I wanted to avoid having to pay for cleaning eight to ten times a month. I've never had a desire to become a maid, janitor or concierge service. If you're looking to get into the STR I would suggest you consider the customer that you want to attract before setting up your business. Then consider the amount of work you are willing to put into running and managing the business. Use the chart below as a guide to decide which type of rental business would be a good fit for you.

Rental Type	Duration	Typical Guests	Needs/Wants
Nightly Rentals	Nightly up to 30 days	Tourists, vacationing families	Home comforts, privacy, amenities
Weekly Rentals	7 days to ~1 month	Workers, low-income tenants	Affordable, safe, near transit
Mid-Term Rentals	1 month to 1 year	Traveling professionals	Quiet, furnished, pet friendly

A typical short-term unit can usually gross at least triple the amount of rent that you could make from an annual lease on the same property. Of course, you must account for additional expenses like furnishings, cleaning, utilities and other expenses. But even after subtracting your operating expenses, this can still be a lucrative endeavor.

For example, I currently own a couple of one-bedroom apartment units that are approximately 400 square feet each. Market rents in my town for those unfurnished units range from $450 – $525 monthly each. Let's just take an average of $500 and compare that same apartment versus nightly, weekly and monthly furnished rentals.

Rental Income Comparison (1-BR Apartment Example)

Rental Type	**Rate**	**Income/Year**
Annual Unfurnished	$500/month	$6,000
Nightly Furnished	$70/night, 90% occupancy	$23,000
Weekly Furnished	$300/week	$15,600
Monthly Furnished	$1,300/month	$15,600

Note: These are my numbers for my units in my market. Your numbers will vary depending on your market.

The STR business has served me well, but it's not all roses. There are a number of challenges that I see today and on the horizon for the STR business. Of course, you will need to do your due diligence and address these before taking the leap into the deep end of the STR pool.

Challenges of Short-Term Rentals

- Finding reliable cleaning & maintenance help
- Competition from hotels
- Market saturation in some areas (thriving near resorts/ natural attractions)
- Neighborhood complaints and HOA restrictions
- Zoning and new regulations limiting STR growth
- Insurance complications (homeowner policies often exclude STR)

LEASE WITH OPTION TO PURCHASE

Someday you may wish to own the property that you are leasing. An option will give you the right to buy the property at some date in the future at a set price. A lease option must be in writing to be enforceable. Also, there must be some consideration – money. The consideration or money doesn't always have to be cash to the seller. Some of the more creative ways to offer consideration could be by paying delinquent mortgage payments; paying for prior code violations; spending money to furnish or fix up the property to make it livable again; there are many alternatives to offering the owner cash. The option must include a price and must be recorded at your local courthouse.

Since you will be entering a long-term business relationship with this person, something akin to marriage, you want to make sure mortgage, taxes and insurance are being paid on time. If the property has a mortgage you will need to be able to communicate with their mortgage company. The mortgage company will not talk to you without an *Authorization to Release* form completed and signed by the seller. You and the seller will need to decide which one of you will be making the mortgage payment going forward. If the seller plans to continue making the mortgage payments, then it's imperative that you trust but verify.

There are a few other things to consider at a minimum when doing a lease option. I highly recommend that you at least address the following and make sure to put them in writing because people get amnesia once they are no longer in pain.

- Who pays the mortgage, taxes and insurance?
- How do each of you get proof of payments for mortgage, insurance, taxes (online).
- Who gets the tax deductions for mortgage interest?
- Who pays for major repairs, roofs, HVAC, etc.? Who pays for minor repairs?
- When, where and how to make the monthly payments?
- Is any of the monthly payment credited towards the purchase price?

- What happens if you can't make the lease payments?
- Do I need to get a new insurance policy?

At a minimum, all these questions need to be addressed and put in writing as part of the lease agreement. Ask me how I know... let me tell you the story about my trials and tribulations from my first attempt at a lease option.

My story about my first lease option.

On my first attempt at a lease option, I ended up coming out very well on the deal in the end. However, I made just about every mistake that could possibly be made on a lease option deal. Mind you, my only coach and guide back then was a book and a set of tapes that I used to do my first lease option deal.

I was all hyped, excited and ready to conquer the world after freshly coming out of a weekend Guru Ballroom Real Estate Seminar. I purchased a guy's course on Lease Options and paid $600.00 for the book and the coursework. That money for the course was not easy to come by so I was determined to go out and find a deal that paid much more than the $600.00 I spent on that course. Unfortunately, I didn't know what I didn't know.

I found my first lease option opportunity by scrolling social media. I located a couple who were struggling to rent out their vacant house. The couple had moved out of state for the husband's job. At first, I conversed with them online and then later talked on the phone.

I found out that they had moved out of state and had no plans to come back to the area. They didn't have enough equity in their house to sell through a realtor, so they decided to rent it out. Apparently, they had rented the place to a family member. The tenant decided that they could no longer afford the house and just stopped making rent payments. The owners were relying on the rent payments to pay their mortgage and eventually got two months behind on their mortgage.

When I reached them on the phone, I simply explained to them that I am an investor, and I want to rent their house. I explained that I would not be moving into the house but would be renting it out at a higher price than their mortgage. I guaranteed them the $500.00 that they were asking for rent, along with an additional $50.00 per month.

Further, I indicated that I would like to purchase the house from them at some point in the future. Also, I didn't want them to sell the house to someone else without my knowledge.

That's the exact language that I used to make the communications clear and understandable to the sellers. I was tempted to utilize some of the big words that I had learned at the Guru Seminar. I knew they wouldn't understand the industry jargon and would become confused. Remember the old saying – "a confused mind says NO!"

My next conversation with them went "we will need to complete the paperwork. We will need three documents to give me permission to rent the house, then rent it out to someone else and ultimately an agreement to buy the house. Those three documents were

(1) my lease from them,

(2) an agreement to sublease, and

(3) an option agreement to purchase at a future date.

The only numbers we discussed were the: (A) monthly rent, which was their $500.00 mortgage plus $50.00 per month; (B) downpayment, which was the option consideration. I paid their two delinquent mortgage payments with late fees for a total of $1,100.00; the final number discussed was the purchase price. Neither of us had any idea what the house would be worth even a year from now. Just as the Guru had taught, I suggested that we make the sale price, sometimes referred to as the strike price, at the "then mortgage balance at the time of closing."

We all agreed to the numbers, and they agreed to meet and sign papers at a restaurant off the interstate the following week. We met very briefly, signed the documents and they were back on the highway. All the way while driving back home I was so elated that I had just gotten a chance to make monthly income from a house that I didn't even own. I spent about three days painting and cleaning and immediately rented it out for $750.00 a month, giving me a $200.00 monthly profit.

Here are the numbers:

- Option Consideration – $1,100.00
- Monthly Payment to Owner – $550.00

- Homeowner Equity – $22,000.00
- Current Mortgage Balance – $49,000.00
- Sale Price – Mortgage balance at time of payoff

We failed to address most of the questions outlined above. The one thing I did right is that I got an Authorization to Release Form signed that allowed me to communicate with their mortgage company. In fact, I got the monthly mortgage set up to draft directly from my bank account monthly to ensure that timely payments were made. I prefer to make the payments directly to the bank, so I never have to worry about the payments being made on time. The taxes and insurance were included in the mortgage so they both were covered also. Did I say insurance was included with the mortgage? Yes, insurance was included but... we kept the homeowners' policy in place and things could have gotten sticky if there had been a claim filed. Once the owners moved out and the property and it became a rental, there should have been a landlord policy placed on the property. Please, cut me a little slack here, I was brand new, again, I didn't know what I didn't know. It only gets worse from here.

Who gets the tax deductions for mortgage interest?

The short answer is whoever both of you agree will receive the mortgage interest tax deduction at the end of the year. Now this little house with a 30-year $60,000 mortgage is not a significant amount of interest paid, especially on a 12-year-old mortgage.

We never thought of discussing it during our negotiations. You guessed it...the homeowner took the annual mortgage interest deduction on their income taxes.

Who pays for major repairs, roofs, HVAC, etc.? Who pays for minor repairs?

We never broached that topic either during our negotiations. I leased that property for almost eight years before buying it. Do you think we had any maintenance calls? Do you think anything broke over that eight-year period? Heck yeah! The roof was already old and needed to be replaced before I leased the place. I paid someone to patch that ragged roof twice after leaks destroyed a ceiling fan and some of the residents' furnishings. The heating and air conditioning system was repaired three times over the years. The built-in oven and water heater were also replaced during that period, just to mention a few. I paid for all those costly repairs plus the usual minor repairs like drain lines, toilets, etc.

A more experienced investor would have thought to discuss who pays for repairs. It is customary in a lease option property for both parties to agree on how major repairs will be handled. For instance, we could have agreed that I would cover all minor repairs, say $200.00 or less. The owner would be responsible for any repairs over that amount. Also, I should have included a clause to address handling major repairs that are needed but the owner doesn't want to pay for. One way to handle that situation is to agree that for every dollar I spend on major repairs, I get that amount deducted from the sales price when I close on that property.

Is any portion of the monthly payment credited towards the purchase price?

It is acceptable and customary for a portion of the rent to be credited towards the purchase price. Again, I didn't know enough to even ask that question.

What happens if you can't make the lease payments?

This is another item that we didn't discuss at all. You want to have this discussion because if I hadn't lived up to my side of the bargain and stopped making payments then what happens. Do we go to an eviction court and treat it as a civil matter, or do we have to foreclose? I've done a lot of reading on this, but I am not going to attempt to answer the question. I just want to make sure you aware that this can become a serious issue if not thought out beforehand. Consult an attorney in your state prior to executing an option agreement.

Do you record your option?

Not all states require that you record your option to purchase contract. My state, North Carolina, requires that the option agreement be recorded. According to my $300.00 hour attorney, the option must be recorded within 14 days of signing and it's the responsibility of the seller to make sure it's recorded. My seller didn't record their option and neither did I. We didn't know at the time that a Memorandum of Option should have been filed at the local courthouse. I only found out when I contacted my seller and said, "I'm ready to exercise my option to buy the property at 123 Main Street." My seller said, "what option?" It took almost another year but my $300.00 per hour attorney did his job!

Do I need to get a new insurance policy on the property?
More than likely, you will need to get a new insurance policy for the property. The Homeowner Policy will not cover the property once the owner moves out and it becomes a rental. However, if you are leasing from an existing landlord, you should be okay to continue their existing policy. Please contact your insurance professional for advice on the proper insurance coverage.

You are probably thinking, "he made almost every mistake imaginable on that lease option deal." You are correct, but I took action! I attempted to apply some of the knowledge that I had gained from that seminar. The deal actually turned out to be profitable in spite of all the mistakes I made with the paperwork. Just remember that real estate is very forgiving ...over time. If you have the time and resources, you can ride out a not so good deal over time and make it very profitable. That's the beauty of options; they allow you to buy at today's prices several years in the future.

Buying on lease option is a good way to pay the owners' asking price for properties even when they are overpriced. The key is to make sure you have a monthly cashflow from the rental income and you can afford to wait long enough until the value goes up before you exercise your option.

Chapter 8:

CONTROL WITHOUT OWNERSHIP: MAKE MONEY BUYING *SUBJECT-TO* EXISTING FINANCING

For years investors have been acquiring properties with little or no money down by taking over payments. Investors were able to assume most mortgage loans without any qualification requirements up until the 1990s. Lenders then stopped allowing loan assumptions by including verbiage in the mortgage documents. The investors gravitated to a lesser-known, more advanced acquisition technique called buying *Subject-to the existing financing*, also known in the industry as *Subject-to* or *Sub2*. The term *Subject-to* is defined as an acquisition technique that allows you as the investor to take over the owner's payment and control the property while the mortgage remains in the seller's name.

The mortgage loan continues to remain in the seller's name until either all payments are made to pay off the loan in full or the property is sold.

Subject-to offers several compelling advantages:

- Control property with little or no money down
- No credit checks or bank approvals required

- Potential for instant equity or cash flow
- Save on loan origination fees and closing costs
- Faster, simpler transactions when handled correctly

This chapter introduces the concept but does not replace proper legal or real estate education. Work with a knowledgeable REIA group and real estate attorney to ensure legal compliance.

Please understand that this is not an attempt to teach you such complex subject matter in a short chapter in this book. Your proper education should come from a REIA group or REIA group-sanctioned training. Your REIA group will help to locate an attorney or title company that will allow subject-to-closings. I estimate that less than 1% of all real estate attorneys will even consider doing a subject-to-closing. If you're not networking with a group, then it's unlikely that you will be able to locate an attorney for your closing.

I will give you an overview of *Subject-to* along with the pros and cons, also will share some of the pitfalls and the reasons some investors get in trouble using the technique.

You, as an investor, can take over a property Subject-to existing financing, which is perfectly legal, when done by an attorney or a title company. There is a line on the Settlement Statement (formerly HUD-1) that says: "Existing Loan(s) Assumed or Taken Subject-to."

Some investors found *Subject-to* as a quick and easy way to build an investment portfolio and make serious money in real estate. The Investors would locate sellers who are in distress and need to get out from under their mortgage payments.

Investors typically target sellers in distress:

- Delinquent on mortgage payments
- Owning multiple properties with unaffordable payments
- Facing relocation or job loss
- Holding overleveraged or repair-needy properties

These situations create motivated sellers willing to transfer property ownership—even while retaining mortgage liability.

In most instances, the seller either (A) owes too much on the property to list and sell with a realtor (B) is making more than one house payment, or (C) owns a property needing major repairs that they can't afford to make in order to sell the property. These scenarios frequently present opportunities for investors to acquire properties Subject-to the existing financing.

A good rule of thumb when considering *Subject-to,* is that the property should either have a monthly cash flow, where the rent exceeds the monthly mortgage, or equity for potential profit upon resale, or both. Make sure there is enough equity so that you can cash a big check when you resell!

You might wonder why anyone would consider transferring title to their property while keeping the mortgage in their name. This situation is what we refer to as a "motivated seller." Motivated sellers typically seek immediate relief, and the Subject-to process allows them to move on quickly. Since the mortgage remains in the seller's name, timely payments made by the buyer can actually improve the seller's credit rating over time.

In some instances, buyers may even allow sellers to remain in the property as renters, so they don't have to move out. Now you can see how or why distressed sellers in any of those situations would be open to someone taking over their existing payments. *Note: Never allow sellers to remain in the property under any circumstances!*

Buying property *Subject-to* is not for the novice investor. At the very least It requires some level of understanding and the use of an attorney to be done properly. I recall when I started investing in the early 2000s, *Subject-to* investing was quite popular. It was all the rage since assumable loans were quietly going away. Investors had to find another way to get into a property with little or no money down.

Some investors used to do what we called "kitchen table closings" back then. The investors would go in, sit down at the kitchen table and they would ask the seller to get the deed. The seller would sign the deed over to the investor and the investor would start making the seller's payments to the mortgage company going forward. They didn't use attorneys or title companies to close on the properties. The loan stayed in the seller's name, but the investor had the deed and was in control of the property.

Common Pitfalls and Risks

Subject-to can be risky if misused. Avoid these common traps:

1. **Missing payments** – You damage the seller's credit and risk foreclosure.

2. **Renting to the seller** – Can cause confusion over ownership.
3. **Sellers expect to get their house back** – Especially if they believe it was a temporary "loan."
4. **Seller remorse** – They may claim fraud or deception.
5. **Improper insurance** – Homeowner's insurance doesn't cover rental properties.
6. **Due-on-sale clause (DOS)** – Lender could call the full loan balance due.

The **Due-on-Sale Clause** allows the lender to demand full repayment if ownership changes. However, if you maintain payments and proper insurance, banks rarely enforce it.

Learning From the Past

There were plenty of horror stories going around back in the early 2000s. Our Attorney General here in North Carolina as well as the Attorneys General in numerous states started cracking down on investors who were using *Subject-to* to prey on unsuspecting homeowners.

I witnessed a couple of egregious cases firsthand, one in North Carolina and the other in Georgia. The North Carolina investor had acquired 53 properties using the Subject-to method. He acquired some of those properties directly from unsuspecting homeowners and others through wholesalers. Unfortunately, the wholesalers had assigned their rights to the investor without the sellers' knowledge. The sellers were left believing that the wholesalers were responsible for making their mortgage payments. After collecting their fees, the wholesalers moved on to new opportunities, while the investor's payment history varied. Several sellers complained to the media and ultimately to the Attorney General. They stated in their complaints that they had not sold their property but had put it up as collateral for a loan from the investor to catch up on their back payments. They were now looking to get back ownership of their property.

I knew one of the complainants who was a sanitation worker at a local municipality. I saw him being interviewed on the local 6 o'clock news. The headline read something like: "Wealthy Real Estate Investor Scams Sanitation Worker and Leaves Family Nearly Homeless."

It was obvious that these were kitchen table closings and were doomed to fail from the beginning. Here is the more likely scenario:

Investors would contact a homeowner who's three months or more behind on their mortgage payments. They would promise to make up the back mortgage payments and continue to make the payments going forward. Some homeowners don't want to leave their homes because they have nowhere to go. The investor would allow the homeowner to rent the property back at a rate that is higher than the monthly mortgage payment. The investor would charge enough rent to cover the monthly mortgage payments and generate some monthly cashflow. The investor benefits from allowing the seller to stay in the property because they don't have to fix up the property nor do they have to go out and find a new tenant.

This arrangement goes on for months or even years with timely mortgage payments being made by the investor. The seller's credit score begins to improve, and with the improved score they are now able to qualify for some bank financing. The seller would then call the investor and say, "I'm ready to pay back the loan that I got from you to catch up my back payments." The investor would then say, "I'm sorry, it's my house, I bought it from you, that wasn't a loan." The seller complains to the media saying, "I borrowed money from this investor and now he wants to take my house." Finally, the state Attorney General gets wind of the investor's activity. The investor had better pray that it's not an election year!

Unfortunately, there will always be those among us who are out to game the system. It saddens me that the few bad actors give the rest of us honest and ethical investors a bad name. Those bad actors cause lawmakers to penalize us all with not-so-well-thought-out legislation.

The other case I read about was an investor in Georgia that had acquired well over a hundred properties that he had taken Subject – to. Things were going well, and he was consistently making the payments until the real estate market crashed in

2008. Most banks stopped lending at that time and real estate values plummeted.

That investor was not able to pay all of those 100+ mortgages that he was now responsible for. He left over a hundred distressed sellers looking for alternatives because they were about to get foreclosures on their credit records. Things can and will go wrong in this business, so I suggest you use good judgement. Subject – to has created fraud problems across the country with folks going out, getting the deed and not making mortgage payments as promised. That is a fraudulent act that could lead to prison time.

Due On Sale Clause

Most mortgage documents include a due-on-sale clause designed to prevent the owner from transferring the property without paying off the underlying mortgage. However, when executed properly, Subject-to financing offers a viable alternative that allows for the legal transfer of the property without triggering this clause.

I just want to make sure I'm clear here, I've never done a Subject-to transaction in all of my 25 years of investing. But the qualified educators and attorneys who teach subject-to will tell you that there is no due on sale jail. I can attest that banks don't care who pays the mortgage payments, they just want the money. Banks are not in the house business; they are in the money business. I have been making mortgage payments and even HELOC payments on properties where the mortgages are in someone else's name. I have been making those payments since 2015 and the bank has accepted each payment, as a matter of fact, they draft the monthly mortgage payments from my account. If I miss a mortgage payment, then I'm sure that the bank will contact the mortgagee, and the mortgagee will in turn call with an unpleasant conversation.

Likewise, investors missing a **subject-to** mortgage payment will get the bank's attention and could trigger the due-on-sale clause. Just by paying the mortgage payment on time as promised will eliminate one of the two most likely due on sale triggers.

The other is not having proper insurance on the property. Think about it, when the seller is living in the house, they have typical homeowners' insurance. Once they move out, their homeowner's insurance is no longer valid because the property is being rented or leased. You, as the investor, must be aware of this and get the proper insurance, which is not easy to find through the typical agent. Never consider leaving the original homeowner's insurance in place while purchasing an additional policy, as this can lead to complications.

Some Subject-to Warnings to New Investors

Subject-to is **not** a beginner strategy. Avoid it if:

- You don't have significant cash reserves
- You don't understand the legal risks
- You don't use an attorney and proper documentation

Note: Never rent the home back to the seller. Never conduct informal closings. Always use professionals.

You will need enough cash to make that mortgage payment, even if your tenant doesn't pay you anything. Remember that you are committed to making that seller's mortgage payments and you must honor that commitment. Therefore, if money is tight and you have the choice between making your personal mortgage payment versus the seller's mortgage payment, you had better make that seller's payment. Yes, it's just that serious!

Chapter 9:

BUYING AND HOLDING RENTALS

While creating quick cash through bird-dogging or wholesaling can be rewarding, real wealth in real estate comes from owning property over time, often referred to as the buy-and-hold strategy. However, buying and holding real estate isn't for everyone. Many of you may have picked up this book because you are broke and lack good credit. Just because you *can* buy a property with little or no money does not mean you *should* buy and hold that property. My biggest caution is this: **Never attempt to hold rental property if you are financially strained!**

You might ask, how much money should I have in reserves if I want to hold rentals? I can't tell you how much you should hold in reserves, but I will tell you how to determine if you are too broke to hold rentals. You are too broke to hold rentals if you are relying on your resident solely to pay the monthly mortgage, taxes, and insurance. In short, if your resident doesn't pay for one month or decides to skip out overnight and you can't pay the mortgage payment, then you are too broke to own rental property!

Your reserves can be in the form of cash in the bank, money in retirement accounts, credit cards, lines of credit, or any other revenue sources that you can tap to cover mortgage payments and repairs without having to borrow the funds in a pinch.

There are ongoing expenses such as insurance, taxes, maintenance, and repairs, just to name a few. If you are broke or financially strapped, your residents can and will begin to quickly sense it and view you as a desperate landlord. Being broke will cause you to make emotional decisions and short-term decisions about things such as maintenance, repairs and resident selection. Operating while broke may cause you to lower your selection criteria to fill a unit to avoid a vacancy. Your property will end up underperforming, and most of your residents will move on to better-managed properties if they can. The less desirable residents will stay and make it difficult to attract quality residents in the future. I find that working with less desirable residents can sometimes cause your attitude to become a bit jaded. That jaded attitude can lead to a scarcity mentality and ultimately lead to a feeling of apathy towards your residents. Unfortunately, apathy is one of the key characteristics of a burnt-out landlord, commonly referred to as a "Slumlord."

Again, rental income over time is the key to wealth. Unfortunately, society seems to think that the very day that you buy your first little rental property you instantly become a millionaire, and you are now rich. Your residents will view you as being rich because you own the $100k house that they are renting from you. They just paid you $1,000.00 for rent and they know that you own 9 other rentals, all paying $1,000.00 each, so that greedy landlord is making $10,000.00 a month on his rentals.

Public perception can be misleading. The average homeowner understands the financial demands of maintaining a single home, and if you manage multiple properties, they may assume you're financially comfortable. Moreover, courts and government entities often treat property owners as though they have deep pockets, forcing you to allow tenants to remain in your units even when they fail to pay the rent.

When I first started buying rentals in the late 1990s, my goal was to have cash flow (profit) of $200.00 per month per unit. Talk about the slow road to wealth...the thought process was that I would net $200.00 per month for 8 years until the property is paid off, and then I would really cashflow more when the mortgage is finally paid off.

Let's look at what happened to every dollar of rent I received with my rentals. Of course, your numbers will vary depending on where you invest. Let's unpack how that $200 actually came to be, and where the rest of the rent money went each month. Your mileage may vary depending on your market, but this was typical for my experience.

Where Each Dollar of Rent Goes

For every $1.00 rent I collected, here's how it usually broke down. Remember, these are my numbers from my rental business. Your numbers may vary:

- **Taxes & Insurance:** ~7%
- **Repairs & Maintenance:** ~4%

- **Capital Expenditures (CapEx):** ~3% (for big-ticket items like HVAC, roof, etc.)
- **Property Management Fees:** ~10%
- **Vacancy ~6%**

That's a total of **~30%** going toward what I like to call "hidden costs." These expenses are easy to forget but very real. And this 30% doesn't even include the mortgage payment yet!

A Typical Rental Example

Let's look at a real-world scenario:

- **Monthly Rent:** $1,000
- **Purchase Price:** $100,000
- **Down Payment:** $20,000 (20%)
- **Loan Amount:** $80,000
- **Interest Rate:** 6%
- **Term:** 30 years
- **Monthly Mortgage Payment:** ~$480
- **30% Operating Costs:** $300

Monthly Cash Flow:

$1,000 (Rent)

- $480 (Mortgage)

- $300 (Operating Costs)

= $220 Net Monthly Income

So, there you have a typical rental that nets **$220/month** after all the usual expenses. Not bad, especially when you stack up multiple properties. It's not get-rich-quick, but it's definitely get-rich-eventually.

Keep this kind of math in mind when analyzing potential rentals. Those "hidden" costs will eat your lunch if you forget to budget for them.

This was a typical example that I used when starting out. Additionally, like many others, I manage my own properties to eliminate the 10% management fee and increase my returns. I shared these numbers to help you understand that a low purchase price doesn't automatically make a property a good buy-and-hold rental investment. I highly encourage you to learn about the property management business before buying your first rental. The rental business has changed, more importantly, people have changed. During my parents' generation people could rent a house with just a handshake, no written lease, just a promise to pay. Even though we were never tenants growing up, I knew several families who lived in rentals. They always made sure they had rent money available to pay on the first of the month. They would pay their rent even if it meant skimping on food and other bills. If the landlord failed to show up on the 1st, they would hunt the landlord down to make sure their rent was paid.

Now, let's go forward to 2025. Our society has become so entitlement-minded and litigious that I now have a 10-page lease along with 8 pages of addenda. Landlord/Tenant Laws vary from state to state, and enforcement varies by jurisdiction. Therefore, the property management business is not as intuitive as some people seem to think. You can no longer go out and buy a house, put someone in it, and happily collect rent for the next 30 years.

I'm sure you have seen or read horror stories about squatters, tenants deliberately destroying properties, and the like. There is no guarantee that this won't ever happen to one of your properties, but there is a lot you can do upfront to reduce the likelihood of ever having those problems with your properties. Get educated and learn from the mistakes of others because we are no longer managing houses and stuff. We are now dealing with managing people and personalities.

Chapter 10:

HOW TO LOCATE THE RIGHT PROPERTIES – THE 4 DS

Wholesalers must buy property at a significant discount, usually at an average price of .55 cents on the dollar or less. We all know that it's very unlikely that any homeowner living in a nice house is willing to sell you their current residence for 55 cents on the dollar unless there are some rare and extreme circumstances. I'm not saying that it will never happen, but it's unlikely that it will happen, especially for you as a novice investor.

Therefore, the properties that we want to target and are most likely to make money on will be those that are vacant and abandoned. Always be on the lookout for vacant houses, especially those that appear to need work.

Identifying abandoned houses is straightforward enough that almost anyone can do it. Experienced investors can often spot a vacant house while driving down a highway or city street at the posted speed limit. Look for telltale signs such as overgrown lawns, damaged siding, boarded-up windows, houses with fire damage, trash in the yard, broken windows, tarps on roofs, or missing electric meters. You can also observe more subtle clues, like mailboxes stuffed with mail, newspapers piled on porches, unpruned driveway bushes or hedges, and garbage cans that appear to have never been moved.

I am observant of houses with metal window awnings or handicap ramps. The handicap ramps are usually an indication that a senior citizen lives on the property and might have some mobility issues. Mobility is one of the two main reasons that people move into nursing homes. So, keep a keen eye out for properties with handicapped ramps. Those ramps could be a leading indicator of a possible profitable payday. As for metal window awnings, I found that they were popular up until the seventies in my area. Senior citizens are one of the groups who still have them in their houses.

VACANT AND ABANDONED PROPERTIES

I began my real estate investment journey by concentrating on vacant properties, and I recommend you do the same. This niche is among the easiest and most profitable for residential real estate investing when starting out.

First, vacant property can quickly become a potential liability for the owner and the community. There are still costs associated with maintaining the property even if it's vacant. The property owner will still be responsible for paying taxes and insurance on the property. Then there is the basic upkeep, lawn care, and keeping the property secured and boarded up to protect against intruders, squatters, vermin, and rodents. There are also concerns about vandalism, fire, and disgruntled neighbors. Let's face it, no one wants to live next door to a vacant boarded-up building. Vacant buildings can attract the worst elements to a neighborhood.

Another advantage for you as an investor is that banks typically won't finance vacant properties, and most insurance companies won't insure them either. They must be bought with cash or bought creatively. Most potential homebuyers don't have wads of cash and need some sort of bank financing. Therefore, homeowners are not going to be able to buy vacant properties and will not be your competition. Your only competition for these properties is from other investors. In most instances, you will be the only one seeking out these properties and making offers to provide relief to the property owners.

Another advantage is that there is less emotional attachment compared to someone having to pack up and move out of their primary residence. Also, most vacant properties don't end up being listed with realtors or the MLS either. Some realtors will refuse to list a rundown abandoned structure because they only want to list pretty properties. They do not want to tarnish their image or brand by listing a run-down structure. Finally, some realtors view it as too much work for such small potential realtor commissions for cheap property.

The key is to encourage the owner of a vacant property to reach out to you. When they call, you're likely their only option at that moment. I often joke with fellow investors that I've bought properties from owners who did not even realize their property was for sale. I say it kind of tongue-in-cheek, but the reality is that when a property initially goes vacant, the owner is concerned and continually thinks about what to do about the vacant property. As time goes on, that owner gets a little more comfortable with the fact that they have vacant property. They rationalize that the place is secure, they pay to keep the grass cut and they pay the taxes every year.

After several years with no vandalism, fires or break-ins, it becomes "out of sight, out of mind." The owners spend less time thinking about the vacant property. Imagine their surprise when, after over ten years of vacancy, they receive a postcard from Gerald stating that he buys houses. This postcard has now reminded them of the liability that they had conveniently forgotten. They picked up the phone and called me. I reopened that wound that had temporarily scabbed over for months or even years in some cases. I do that by reminding them of all the bad things that could potentially happen to that vacant property. I further make sure that they understand that they will be able to sleep much better at night once this liability is out of their lives for forever. Those potential issues had always existed, but the owner had conveniently put them on the back burner and had gotten them off their minds. They end up selling me their problem property on cash or terms. Again, I have no other competition, and I present a solution to their problem.

Situational Sellers –

An easy way to find situational sellers is through attorneys. Here is the story on a very cheap property that I found through an attorney.

Networking With Attorneys: *the Cheapest House I Ever Bought*

The cheapest property I ever bought came from a lead generated by an estate attorney. As I mentioned earlier, I mailed letters to estate attorneys, made phone calls, and even dropped by their offices for cold calls. I found that attorneys have no emotional attachment, whatsoever, to a property, and are the consummate, disinterested third parties. My experience with some attorneys is that they will sell a property for less than 20 cents on the dollar if they can justify it, but it must always sell for enough to get their legal fees.

One strategy that served me well was pursuing their paralegals and building rapport with them. Attorneys are usually incredibly busy and bill their time in 15-minute increments, making it unlikely that they will meet with you just to hear about your services. So, when I call or visit an attorney's office, I always ask for Attorney Jones's paralegal, as they are the gatekeepers.

I had sent several mailings to this attorney over time. Her paralegal finally picked up the phone one day and called me with a lead. My attorney mailings emphasize that I am interested in purchasing less-than-desirable properties, or properties that are so ugly that realtors don't want to list. The paralegal called me about this one-acre farm lot that had a small house on it.

The house had been vacant for at least 20 years, so long that trees had grown up through it and it was no longer visible from the road. Apparently, the elderly lady who owned it had been in a nursing home for 20 years before she passed.

When the paralegal called and said, "Mr. Honeyblue, your letter states that you will buy houses in any condition. Well, we have a doozy for you." I could hear her chuckle. I went out and looked at the property and never attempted to enter the small house because it was so over-grown with trees, bushes, and weeds. I created some bandit signs and posted them at the 4 nearest intersections. The handwritten sign said "$12k, Mobile Home Lot, W/ Well & Septic, 919.555.555." This is one of the few times that I mention bandit signs in this book because bandit signs are illegal in most jurisdictions. Have I used bandit signs before, other than this one instance? Have I received calls from city and county zoning and code enforcement about illegal signs? Please check your local laws before placing any signs on public property or public rights-of-way.

Afterward, I returned to the attorney's office and signed the purchase and sale agreement. They held the agreement in suspense because they had to advertise in the local newspaper for a 10-day upset bid period. During the 10-day period, my phone rang off the hook from buyers looking for a mobile home lot. I closed the property for $2,400.00 and sold it for $12K about two weeks later to a firefighter who wanted the lot because it was right next door to his ailing grandmother.

The 4 Ds and How to Search and Locate

As discussed in earlier chapters, you can drive through neighborhoods to locate distressed properties by observing their condition from the street. Another effective approach is to identify situational sellers, those experiencing circumstances that compel them to sell their property at a steep discount for relief.

You'll have to spend some money on marketing to find situational sellers. Situational sellers are the four categories of property owners that we call the 4-Ds.

I will briefly discuss each of these and explain where to search and find them.

1. Debt
2. Disability
3. Divorce
4. Death

1ST DEBT

We'll start with debt. Various financial situations can lead a person to fall behind on mortgage payments, ranging from living beyond their means, job loss, to facing legal costs or even an active prison sentence. There will always be individuals who cannot or will not pay their mortgage for various reasons.

Typically, the mortgage company will file notifications at the local courthouse when a property owner gets 60 – 90 days behind on their mortgage. If you know where to look you can typically search and find pre-foreclosures on your county website. In my state, North Carolina, that information is in the Register of Deeds department with the local county. It's public information so anyone should be able to access the information in person or online. If you don't have online access, then you will just have to make a trip down to your county courthouse. You can also buy a mailing list of homeowners who are 30 – 60 – 90 days late on their mortgages.

It's essential to understand that the foreclosure process varies from state to state. Some states are judicial, requiring lenders to file a lawsuit to foreclose, while others are non-judicial, allowing lenders to proceed without court intervention. Currently, one state has enacted specific laws regarding investors contacting homeowners in foreclosure. If you plan to market to foreclosures, I encourage you to research your state's foreclosure process thoroughly.

The other major debt that happens is bankruptcy. Bankruptcy is a federal law that people who file bankruptcy either reorganize their debts under Chapter 13 or eliminate their debts under Chapter 7. Since bankruptcy is federal, it's consistent from state to state and it's much easier to research. It's not uncommon for homeowners facing foreclosure to file Chapter 13 bankruptcy to stop the foreclosure. However, for some homeowners, this is just a temporary stop-gap measure because a good percentage of them will ultimately fall behind again on their mortgages and eventually lose their homes. The state of North Carolina has a 10-day redemption period after the date of the sale. It is not uncommon for the homeowner to file bankruptcy within that 10-day period even after the high bidder has been acknowledged at the courthouse steps. I recommend that you become familiar with your state's foreclosure procedure and redemption period if you choose to buy foreclosures at the courthouse steps.

Again, bankruptcy is a federal law, and you can access bankruptcy data on the federal government website. You may also network with bankruptcy attorneys to locate potential deals in your area.

Here is a brief story about a deal I bought from a homeowner who was a couple months behind on payments.

I Once Bought a House for Cigarette Money

I must be honest with you, it's not what you think. I didn't pull out a pack of cigarettes and say, "Hey, I'll swap you this pack for your nice brick house." There's much more to the story, and here's how it goes.

I was browsing an online marketplace buy and sell site, searching through rental housing, hoping to find a desperate or burned-out landlord willing to sell on favorable terms. I ran across this one lady who stated in the ad that she wanted to rent her property for the exact cost of her monthly mortgage. The ad reeked of desperation, and as an investor, it was music to my ears.

I messaged her, and she explained that she had moved several states away for a new relationship and was renting out the house.

Unfortunately, the tenants had stopped paying rent and had been living there for at least a few months without paying any rent. Financially strapped, she was struggling to support her new family while unable to afford the trip back to legally evict the tenants. She had been using the rent to cover the mortgage but had now fallen two months behind on payments and was facing the possibility of foreclosure. She agreed to rent the house to me if I paid to catch up on the three back mortgage payments of a little more than $1,500 total. She also agreed to sign an option agreement allowing me to purchase the property at the mortgage balance owed at the closing time. The property immediately cash flowed at least $200 per month after expenses, and I still hold that property today.

By the way, what about the pack of cigarettes? When I started prepping the property I was having a difficult time finding help with cleanup and painting. A local landscaper friend told me about his grandson, Brandon, who was looking for some part-time work. Brandon appeared to be in his late twenties—a clean-cut guy who had taken up painting in Job Corps or trade school. He was a good worker and conscientious and unlike most youngsters his age he wasn't on his cell phone all day. His only obvious vice was that he smoked cigarettes. However, Brandon was a polite smoker: he never smoked inside and only lit up during breaks, carefully disposing of his cigarette butts.

One day while on break, he looked up at me and asked, "Man, do you mind me asking, how much did you pay for this nice brick house?" I was taken aback for a moment and needed to pause before answering. In all my years, I've never had a tradesman, laborer, or anyone else working for me ask how much I paid for a property. Most probably assumed I was wealthy and simply wrote a check to buy each property in cash. It wasn't just Brandon's question but the tone in which he asked it; it felt like he was trying to figure out if he, too, could someday own rental properties.

I replied, "Brandon, I noticed you're a smoker, and cigarettes are very expensive. Let me ask you this: how much do you spend on cigarettes?" He immediately responded, "I spent $972 on cigarettes last year." I then told him exactly what I paid to take over the property, a little over $1,500. He exclaimed, "Wow! I spent more than that on cigarettes in the last 24 months!"

Brandon realized that he could have bought that house by quitting smoking and saving his cigarette money for 18 months. So, I ask you: do you have consumption habits or are vices costing you the opportunity to become wealthy over time?

2ND DISABILITY.

A disabled person is an individual that has been deemed unable to work and earn a living because of a health condition or because of permanent physical injury. Those individuals typically receive monthly income for a lifetime.

The disability check could come from the federal government or from an agency such as a workers' compensation check for work-related injury. Unfortunately, those monthly checks do not usually increase annually or adjust for inflation. Because of inflation, it becomes difficult after a few years for the recipients to make house payments and keep up with their other bills. I once read a statistic that nearly 80% of homeowners on disability will ultimately lose their properties to foreclosure. Typically locating these people will require networking, marketing and word of mouth.

The other disability that you should consider is those individuals who are going to nursing homes or moving in with family for more intensive care. As I mentioned earlier, I keep an eye out for properties equipped with handicapped ramps, as this often indicates that the homeowner is aging and may have mobility issues. The property might ultimately have to be sold once the homeowner either moves in with family, friends or relatives or goes to a nursing home. I'm not aware of any online resources or databases that would compile this data. Disability is the only one of the four Ds that is not recorded in the local courthouse. There are investors who network with nursing homes and assisted living facilities directly to get leads on residents who may need to sell their properties to pay their bills while they're in the nursing home. So that would be one source of identifying potential disability deals.

How I Bought a House with a $1 Million Lien for Under $10K

I spotted a nice small, abandoned house that had been vacant for years. The house wasn't in the best neighborhood, but I could tell that it had been renovated, and the major systems upgraded. The roof looked less than 10 years old. It had vinyl replacement windows, and the electrical system had been upgraded. I could tell all this from the outside and peeping into the windows.

Curious about the property's ownership, I went to the courthouse and discovered an estate attorney was managing it. Upon reviewing the file, I found a document from the state of North Carolina indicating that a bill owed to a nursing home exceeded $1 million. I thought to myself, there's no way this bill is ever going to be paid. I didn't know at the time but later found that when indigent people get older and go into a nursing home, they pledge their property to Medicaid in exchange for paying for their nursing home care. Typically, they will file a lien against the property and sell it to pay the nursing home bill once that person is deceased.

Talk about fishing in your own pond! My curiosity led me to contact the Medicaid folks locally, and my objective was to get as much upfront information as possible and get a better understanding of the process.

I was able to conclude the following from my conversation with the Medicaid collections folks. They know that the property's been vacant for years and has deferred maintenance. This alone makes it only worth pennies on the dollar. They usually rely heavily on local attorneys to get the property sold at a reasonable price.

I called the attorney and arranged a walkthrough of the house. She brought her husband along for security, given that a few men were loitering on the corner. After the walkthrough, I looked at the attorney and said, "Fifty K and a flak jacket." She stared at me in disbelief and asked, "What?" I replied, "NO, I will charge YOU $50,000 and a flak jacket to take this property off your hands." We all shared a laugh before continuing our tour. Ultimately, we agreed on a price of less than $10,000—less than 1% of the $1 million owed to Medicaid. Both the attorney and Medicaid accepted the offer.

Here is the good part: after the attorney and her husband left the house that day, I was still walking around outside checking things over. A guy was standing on the corner and he approached me and started asking questions about the house. He said he was interested in buying the house and he wanted to use his GI Bill benefit to purchase it. We agreed on a price of $29,900.00. I could hardly believe the timing of it all. I already have a buyer for a house that I don't even have under contract yet, and I stand to make a quick $20,000.00.

This was my first time purchasing a nursing home property. Since then, I've done several deals, with that attorney and others.

3RD DIVORCE

We know that divorce is when a married couple decides to end their marriage for some reason or just for no reason. I mentioned earlier in the book that it's extremely rare for someone living in a house that's in good condition to sell their pretty house for 55 cents on the dollar or less. Well, divorce is one of those rare instances I've heard of stories of investors who were able to buy half ownership, 50% ownership in properties where one spouse literally gave away their share of the property for pennies on the dollar just to spite the other spouse or to get back at them.

For some people a divorce can become so emotionally charged that it causes one or both spouses to think and act irrationally. This is where you, as an investor, can come in and help them dispose of the property during those trying times. You stand to make a lot of money if you can deal with the personalities involved. I personally have never worked or purchased a divorce property, but the information is readily available online and at your local courthouse.

4TH DEATH

Probate is a legal proceeding opened when a person dies owning real property. The property is left to the heirs by will, or sometimes there is no will. The heirs will decide if they want to sell the property or to keep the property. The law requires a personal representative or attorney to settle the estate. In short, they must advertise in the legal section of the newspaper to notify creditors that their family member is deceased. Anyone with a claim against the deceased will have to notify the estate at the mailing address listed in the ad. The ad is run for a few weeks and is generally the first notification to the public that someone has died.

My first deal, the "T-Shirt Property," was a probate deal that I bought on land contract. There were a couple of things that stood out from that deal were: (1) the original owners had passed away and left the property to their children; (2) their children didn't live on the property, so they didn't have the emotional attachment that usually comes from "selling our home."

I started going through the Legal Section of numerous local newspapers and started writing letters to those names I saw in the newspaper. The same info from the legal section of the newspaper is also on file in the local courthouse.

However, the courthouse file is much more extensive. It includes a form that lists all assets, including real property as well as names and addresses of all of the heirs. I began going to the local courthouse on my lunch break or whenever I could get away during work. Those files contained all the information I needed to determine if the deceased person owned real property. It was information that people had to search out and find so it was not easily accessed by the masses. I quickly realized that I had found a secret fishing hole that no one else knew about except me.

When I couldn't get to the courthouse, I would browse the legal ads in several online newspapers. In other words, I'd go and look at an online newspaper, flip over to the classifieds, and I would pull all the names of deceased people from the newspaper. Then I would cross-reference the names with the county tax rolls to see if they owned any real property. You can easily do the same if you can't get to the courthouse during business hours.

Probate became such a niche for me that I researched probate properties in about 20 counties. I knew I could not handle those 20 counties alone, so I subcontracted with a courthouse researcher to pull the leads for me. At one point I hired a friend's daughter to pull leads while she was in college at the courthouse in her county. I used to have a virtual Assistant (VA) to do the data entry for me, and I even once had a live answering service for all incoming calls. However, I printed and mailed the letters myself because I didn't trust anyone else with this task.

Here is one of the many probate deals that I've done over the years. I tell this story because I bought it from an heir who had only seen the property once. She just wanted it gone and we obliged her. We still hold this property today as a rental.

$10K for A Nice Brick House on an Ugly Block

I received a call from a young lady in New York City in response to one of my letters regarding a house she had inherited. She said, "I will take $10,000 for the house. Go and look at it and let me know." I tried to engage her in conversation in an effort to build a rapport, but she wasn't interested. All she shared was that it was a three-bedroom, one-bath brick house, along with the address. Since I didn't recognize her name and couldn't recall sending her a letter, I didn't press her for more information.

The property was over an hour away, but I promptly headed out the next morning and went by to look at the property. It was a nice house on an ugly street but the minute I saw the house I realized that $10,000 was a steal for that house even in its current condition. The roof looked less than five years old, there were vinyl replacement windows all around and the electrical had been upgraded from fuses to breakers. Additionally, the high-end HVAC gas package unit was only six years old.

The interior only needed painting, deep cleaning, and carpet cleaning. It did appear that someone had locked a dog in the bathroom for a considerable period of time. So the bathroom needed to be cleaned out and washed down before painting.

When I pulled up to the house, I immediately called the young lady and offered her $10,000. I told her I would overnight a Purchase & Sale Agreement for her signature.

I was perplexed; I could not figure out why the young lady was willing to sell that property for considerably less than its value. I knew she lived about 10 hours away up north, but she could have easily contacted a realtor to list this property and sell it for top dollar.

Now, for the backstory.

I spoke with a neighbor and later found that the house belonged to an elderly woman who had inherited it from her father. After retiring from her nursing job up north, she moved back into the house. The old woman had no children to care for her, so a neighbor across the street took it upon herself to look after her. This neighbor eventually became the administrator of the old woman's estate after her passing. I had mailed my usual probate letter to the neighbor, who then passed it on to the sole heir living ten hours away. This heir was believed to be a grandniece who had little interest in a property so far away, especially since she had only seen it once as a child. Moreover, she had recently discovered she was the sole heir to $166,000 in cash, along with other insurance proceeds.

I briefly considered wholesaling the place for a quick $10,000.00 but ultimately decided to keep it and add it to my portfolio as a long-term rental. I paid a clean-out company $2,700 to cut back the bushes, pressure wash the exterior, clean out the junk inside, and remove the dog residue from the bathroom. We spent another $600.00 on interior painting and carpet cleaning, which means we had less than $14k in the property before being rented.

We still hold that property today.

We have covered the 4-Ds, and you now see that visually chasing abandoned properties—by driving for dollars—is an excellent way to start, especially if you lack a marketing budget. However, to become successful in this real estate game, you will have to stop chasing properties and start pursuing situations. Start fishing where you are the only one at the pond. I'm willing to bet you that every day of our lives, someone is going to miss a house payment, someone will become disabled, some couple will decide to get a divorce, and lord knows someone dies every single day. There will always be an infinite supply of opportunity for as long as we know where to fish.

Chapter 11:

HOW TO WALK A PROPERTY – A QUICK VISUAL INSPECTION

If you are not experienced with construction, then I highly recommend that you get a contractor, handyman, inspector, or someone working in the trades to walk through the properties with you, at least until you get comfortable checking out systems and estimating repairs. Most of my residential construction knowledge came from working all those nights and weekends helping my father build our house. Those very same grueling construction tasks that I resented every single week were the tasks that provided me with the knowledge and ability to walk through a house, evaluate the systems, and estimate repairs accurately within a few short minutes.

Here are some of the things I look for at a property. This is not an exhaustive list, nor is it a substitute for a professional home inspection; it simply provides the basics to get you started, even as a novice. Also, keep in mind that I avoid attics and crawl spaces entirely. At most, I'll peek into those areas with a flashlight for a few seconds. I leave thorough inspections of attics and crawl spaces to the end buyer.

THE ROOF

Start by examining the roof from the ground. Look for tarps or patches, which are obvious indicators of potential problems. All shingles should be lying flat. Look closely at the shingles to determine if they are cupped, curled, or missing, and that would give you some indication of the roof from the outside. Once inside, you can look at the ceilings for leaks, water stains, sagging, or any other signs that might indicate roof leaks.

As I mentioned before, I don't typically go into attics. If there's a pull-down stair and it's convenient, I'll poke my head up to look. My main focus is checking for water stains on the underside of the roof, which could indicate leaks, and making sure the attic is insulated. You can always have a professional inspect the roof at a later time.

FLOORS AND FOUNDATION

Walk the floors in each room as much as possible and be observant for soft spots, or mushy spots. Pay particular attention to floors in the bathrooms and kitchens where there are water sources. Make sure to step on both sides of bathroom toilets, as these are usually some of the most vulnerable areas to moisture. Also, check under sink cabinets for signs of moisture or water damage.

While walking inside the house, look for uneven or warped floors. If the house is carpeted, don't hesitate to find an isolated corner to pull the carpet back (with the owner's permission) to see the surface underneath.

If you are feeling adventurous, open the crawl space door if it's accessible. I usually check for standing water or moisture under the house, the presence of floor insulation, and whether there is a moisture barrier (plastic) covering the ground.

PLUMBING

Typically, most plumbing is hidden behind the walls, but again, you look for evidence of leaks, water stains, water damage, which can all be indicators of the condition of the plumbing. Some areas of the country have boilers but here in the south we typically have water heaters. Look at the water heater piping and see if it appears to have been installed by a professional plumber or is it something just pieced together by a neighbor's brother-in-law.

ELECTRICAL

Your initial check of the electrical system can be done outside when you look at the electric meter to determine if the power is still on. Some jurisdictions will remove the meter when the power is disconnected, but others will leave the meter in place. I've also found that most jurisdictions will require an electrical inspection if the power has been turned off for more than a few months. The inspection will have to be done by the local city/county inspector or a licensed electrician. There will be some costs associated with the inspection.

You want to look in the panel check to make sure that the panel box has breakers and not fuses. The presence of fuses is not a deal breaker but just means that the electrical panel will possibly need to be updated to breakers at some point. Some lenders will not lend money on a property that has fuses and has not been upgraded.

Secondly, make sure that the panel is properly rated for the electrical load. I typically look to see if the panel is a 200 AMP panel, which is a code requirement in most areas. There will typically be a label on the panel as to the amperage so it's not that difficult to figure out.

Wiring, just like plumbing, is hidden behind the walls and is usually not visible during a walk-through. Be observant of any wires that you see to ensure that they look like they were installed by a licensed professional.

HEATING, VENTILATION, AND AIR CONDITIONING

You want to look to make sure that there is a heat and/or cooling source at the property. Next, you will need to determine whether the source is electrical, gas or both. Then look for vents in the house to make sure that there is a vent in every room. Every HVAC system will have a nomenclature tag or label showing the model number, the manufacture date, serial number, capacity, and other information. I generally assume that the unit is not functional in a vacant property, and I include the HVAC replacement in my repair estimate to be on the safe side.

Again, this wasn't meant to be a full-blown home inspection but just the basics that you as a wholesaler could use as a guide for determining the condition of a property. If you get comfortable reviewing just these five systems as a wholesaler, then you will be adding tremendous value to your end buyers. It makes their job easier and would allow you to move your property faster, thereby making you a lot more money.

Chapter 12:

WHERE TO FIND THE FUNDING FOR YOUR DEALS

In the real estate business, there will be times when you need access to capital. Earlier in this book, I outlined how you can get started with little to no money. However, if you truly want to grow and scale your business, securing funding becomes essential.

Where do you find the money to buy and hold property for rental? That's one of the biggest questions I get all the time. I recall when I first got started in real estate and I kept hearing folks at the investor meetings: "Find a deal and the money will come." As a novice investor, I didn't believe it until I actually found a good deal. That's an absolute truth worth repeating. If you find a good deal, you won't have much of a problem finding someone to invest in that deal with you.

Let's delve further into ways to fund our real estate investment deals. I will start with my favorite funding method and go down the list in order of my preference. I will explain each type of financing along with the pros and cons. Again, this is simply my personal hierarchy of preferences.

1. Owner Financing
2. Land Contract/ Contract for Deed
3. Private Money
4. Hard Money
5. Small Local Banks & Credit Unions
6. Large National Banks

SELLER FINANCING

My absolute favorite way of funding real estate deals is owner financing. Yes, the person who's selling me the house will allow me to make payments directly to them. I ask them to become the bank, and I will make monthly payments directly to them rather than going out and getting a loan from a bank. It has, by far, been the best way to fund our deals. Some of the other advantages might be

- no upfront loan fees
- no loan application
- no credit check

SELLER NAMES THE PRICE; I NAME THE TERMS

To put it succinctly, "price is important, but terms are critical." Without favorable terms, low-money or no-money deals simply wouldn't be feasible. When most of us hear the word "terms," we often think of buying a used car. The salesman typically asks, "How much money down, and how much per month?" A skilled used car salesman understands money, compound interest, and financing. Moreover, they know the absolute lowest price at which they can sell the car while still making a profit.

Used car salespeople are much more sophisticated than the typical home seller when it comes to selling. For this reason, I ask that you vow right here and now to never use any techniques in this book to deliberately take advantage of any seller. We talk about win-win deals, where both you and the seller leave the closing table happy with the terms of the deal. Trust your gut on this one, your gut will let you know if you have taken advantage of the seller. Your gut will also let you know if you're making a bad deal and will come out on the losing end of the transaction.

Even the most unsophisticated will ultimately figure out if they are being ripped off or getting the bad side of a deal. Here are some of the things that a seller might say if they don't feel they're getting a fair deal:

- "Give me some time to think about it..."
- "I need my lawyer to look over it..."
- They seem to have questions but are hesitant to ask you those questions.
- They appear to be stalling or trying to wait you out.
- "I need my spouse/child/etc. to look over it."

Remember, a confused mind usually says "no." Some gurus teach students to come up with canned responses to those objections. I don't advocate doing that because the seller might really be confused, and you are just compounding your problem.

I will generally say "Mr./Ms. Seller, I've explained our options as best I could. Is there something that you don't feel comfortable with, price, terms or are you just not comfortable with me? I won't be offended if you tell me that you are not comfortable with me or my offer." I would prefer that the seller let me know this during the negotiation process, rather than ghost me after the contract is signed.

When dealing with the property owner as the bank, everything is negotiable. This includes:

- Downpayment
- Interest Rate (or even 0%)
- Monthly Payment
- Number of Payments
- Start Date of Payments
- End Date of Payments
- Balloon Payment
- Closing Costs
- Closing Date
- Purchase Price
- Total Cost (Principal and Interest)

I have never had a seller ask me my credit score or even inquire as if they were trying to qualify me financially to buy their property. In fact, in over 25 years, it has never happened. By the time I reach the negotiation stage, my credibility is usually established. Like banks, sellers are looking for trust, character, and collateral. When you're negotiating an owner-financing deal, the seller has likely already determined that you are a credible buyer and they trust that you will do what you say.

Owner financing is the number 1 tool in my funding toolbox. It's a very, very powerful tool, but it's not for every seller. After years of doing owner-financed deals I can now pretty much guess who's a likely candidate to finance a deal for me. It's virtually impossible to get owner financing from an owner who lives in a nice house who's having financial difficulties and can't make the payments. The seller must be open to taking payments over an extended period of time.

SELLER FINANCING – NO DOWN PAYMENT

Another critical variable with an owner-financed deal or any deal is the amount of the down payment. Sometimes, a seller may insist on a down payment and won't agree to anything less. I've encountered this situation numerous times. In many cases, however, I've been able to negotiate so that the cash down payment counts toward an equivalent number of monthly payments.

For example, you are negotiating with a seller, and the owner agrees to finance this deal for you with monthly payments of $600 a month. However, this seller insists that you have some skin in the game and says they want a $3,000 down payment.

What you can do is negotiate with the owner by saying something like, "I'll be taking over this property and investing money to fix it up. Instead of a $3,000 down payment, how about we credit that amount toward the first five monthly payments of $600 each? That way, my first payment to you wouldn't be due for five months." This is one of the strategies you can use with owner financing. I've done this many times—I've even negotiated up to six months with no payments and no down payment on owner-financed deals

SELLER FINANCING – ZERO PERCENT INTEREST RATE

One of the things I like is that the sales price and terms of the deal are whatever you and the seller agree to. In most instances I'm able to get zero percent interest, now how powerful is that? As far as I've been able to ascertain, I've never found any other credible lending source where you can get a zero percent interest loan, even with mom and dad. Here is the kicker, if they insist on interest you can agree to pay simple interest rather than compound interest like most bank mortgages.

The money saved by paying simple interest could allow you to pay off the property in less than half the time. Albert Einstein once said, "Compound interest is the eighth wonder of the world," and I tend to agree because compound interest can exponentially grow your wealth. I prefer to buy with simple interest and sell with compound interest.

It is very important to understand the impact interest rates can have on your deal. A high interest can sometimes be the difference between a good deal and a great deal. I highly recommend that you familiarize yourself with some sort of mortgage calculator. A mortgage calculator will come in handy when analyzing a deal, whether with a seller or a lending institution. You may wish to run some "what if" scenarios to determine the impact of additional principal payments on your loan, allowing you to strategically pay down your loan.

For example, we took a $100,000 loan and calculated the payments at various interest rates ranging from 4% to 12%. We amortized those rates and compared them at 15-, 20- and 30-year intervals. You will want to know how much your money is costing you monthly and over the life of the loan.

Take a look at the chart below to see the difference in monthly payments based on various rates and terms. The shaded columns show the total mortgage interest paid over the life of each loan.

Monthly Mortgage Payment Amount & Total Interest Paid by Interest Rate

Interest Rate	15-Year Monthly P&I	15-Year Total Interest Paid	20-Year Monthly P&I	20-Year Total Interest Paid	30-Year Monthly P&I	30-Year Total Interest Paid
4%	$739.00	$33,143.00	$606.00	$45,435.00	$477.00	$71,870.00
5%	$791.00	$42,343.00	$660.00	$58,389.00	$537.00	$93,256.00
6%	$844.00	$51,894.00	$716.00	$71,943.00	$600.00	$115,838.00
7%	$899.00	$61,789.00	$775.00	$86,072.00	$655.00	$139,508.00
8%	$956.00	$72,017.00	$836.00	$100,745.00	$734.00	$164,155.00
10%	$1,075.00	$93,429.00	$965.00	$131,605.00	$878.00	$215,925.00
12%	$1,200.00	$116,030.00	$1,101.00	$164,260.00	$1,029.00	$270,300.00

Data based on a $100,000 mortgage. All numbers have been rounded to the nearest dollar. Does not include taxes and insurance.

I always want to know exactly how much borrowed money is costing me. I was once in total shock when I bought a $150,000 house and looked at the paper amortization schedule they gave me at closing. After I made the first monthly payment of over $1,000.00, only a mere $97.00 went towards paying down the principal on that $150k loan!

Take a look at the chart below where we took the monthly payments from the prior table and separated the interest and principal for the first monthly payment only. The shaded columns show the amount of the payment that goes toward paying down principal.

Monthly P&I Breakdown by Interest Rate

Interest Rate	15-Year Monthly P&I	15-Year Principal Payment	15-Year Interest Payment	30-Year Monthly P&I	30-Year Principal Payment	30-Year Interest Payment
6%	$844.00	$344.00	$500.00	$600.00	$99.55	$499.44
7%	$899.00	$315.00	$583.00	$665.00	$82.00	$583.00
8%	$956.00	$289.00	$667.00	$734.00	$67.00	$667.00

Owner financing is so powerful that I ask for owner financing on every deal I do. Yes, I make an owner finance offer 100% of the time. Am I successful every time? No, but I am successful much of the time. I've done a lot of owner finance deals and that's one way to really expand your wealth in this business.

CLOSER LOOK AT LENDING SOURCES

Let's compare owner financing to typical financing options at traditional lending institutions. For instance, if you're approaching a lender to secure a loan for purchasing rental property, there are several key factors to consider. First, we need to look at the down payment and the interest rate. Next, we want to consider points in relation to the interest rate. We want to know the loan itself—how many years that loan is amortized over. For instance, you could get an adjustable-rate loan for 5%, but it's amortized over 30 years, which means that the monthly payments that you are going to make will be based on 30 years, and at the end of five years, that loan would be adjusted, the rate would go higher, or it would go lower.

Those are the typical aspects we consider when evaluating a rental loan. However, it's important to note that most of these terms are not negotiable with traditional lenders as they are with the owner. Instead, banks offer a range of loan products, each with specific requirements. One loan might require 5% down, another up to 20%, and some could even offer 0% down. Each loan product will specify the interest rates, points, terms, and other details. You may compare three or four different loan products, each slightly different. However, you cannot mix and match features as you would in a cafeteria-style selection. For example, if loan product #1 offers 0% down and loan product #2 requires 20% down but has a lower interest rate, you can't take the interest rate from one and the down payment from another.

In other words, you cannot customize these loan features; they are generally not negotiable with lenders.

In contrast, with owner financing, all these terms are negotiable. As I often state, it all depends on the agreement between you and the owner. Let's start with the down payment, for instance, the down payment. Typically, sellers want a down payment because they expect you, as the borrower, to have some skin in the game. This means they want you to invest something in the project to discourage you from simply walking away and leaving them to take it back. If a seller is insistent on a down payment, it may indicate that they lack confidence in your ability to follow through on the agreement, which is a red flag.

Ideally, you want to acquire property with zero down payment or as small a down payment as possible. It's not uncommon to buy abandoned properties with no money down or zero down payment.

The interest rate can be whatever you and the seller agree upon. In many cases, you could negotiate a 0% interest rate. If the seller insists on charging interest, remember that the interest doesn't have to be compound interest. You can propose simple interest instead. Moreover, there is no law requiring you to pay interest with every installment; consider deferring the interest payments to the end of the loan, making interest part of your final payments.

Traditional lenders will usually charge you points up front—where a point equals 1% of the loan. However, with owner financing, sellers are unlikely to charge points unless they have been advised otherwise.

I like the flexibility of choosing my monthly payments. You can negotiate whatever payment terms work for both parties. Personally, I aim to pay off all of my properties in a reasonable timeframe. To calculate my monthly payment, I divide the total price of the property by 100, which generally corresponds to about eight years. For example, if I purchased a $70,000 property, I'd propose paying $700 a month for 100 months. In less than ten years, that property will be paid off.

Traditional banks typically give you a few weeks' grace period before the first monthly payment is due. When negotiating with an owner you can agree to monthly payments, quarterly payments, or even one annual lump sum payment. Alternatively, you might decide to make a single payment after two or three years. Again, all these terms are negotiable and should be considered when discussing the agreement with the seller. Don't forget closing costs and closing dates; they too are negotiable.

THE PRIVATE MONEY ADVANTAGE

Private money is essentially where individuals who have money to lend, particularly retirement accounts like 401ks, IRAs, and other investment accounts where their money is not earning the rate of return that they would like. The individual lends their money to investors to finance real estate deals and make better returns on their money. Interest rates and terms are very negotiable with private money. They typically are whatever the borrower and lender agree on.

Private money is a quick way to build wealth, especially if you are a rehabber or flipper. Private money lenders typically don't want to tie up their money any longer than 6 to 12 months max. They would prefer to lend their money out where they can turn it by lending it out several times over the course of a year.

The primary advantage of private money is that it can be reasonably cheap money and can be accessed quickly, within hours allowing you to close a deal quickly. Your typical bank loan will take a minimum of 30 to 45 days to close. In some cases, with private money, you could find a deal and close it in less than 7 days, depending on how quickly the title search can be completed. I've seen rehabbers close a deal with private money, do a quick rehab, and have the property back on the market in 6 weeks, which is less time than it takes to close a loan at a typical bank.

Having quick access to guaranteed capital allows you to make offers more confidently. Moreover, being able to claim that you can close a deal in just a few days is a powerful negotiation tool, especially when dealing with extremely motivated sellers, those facing situations that compel them to sell quickly. In most cases being able to close in 7 days or less entitles you to much more of a discount from sellers, especially those sellers who need cash right away. It allows the seller to feel secure that their property won't be sitting there 30, 45 days waiting for a maybe, or waiting for the buyer's bank to agree to fund the deal. The seller can have the transaction completed and move on with their lives.

Another big advantage of private money is you can borrow enough money to cover the entire cost of the transaction. This could cover the cost of purchasing the property, including closing costs, the cost of repairs, and holding costs. Private money could enable you to buy and rehab property without having one penny of your money in the deal. You simply pay back the money when you sell the property.

If you decide to hold the property long-term as a rental, then you can refinance the property and pay back the private loan. I do suggest that you have your refinance lender lined up in advance before purchasing the property.

PRIVATE MONEY LENDERS AND BORROWERS

I refer to private lending as *relationship* lending, but not *casual* lending.

Even though you are doing business with someone you know, like, and trust, it's up to both the lender and borrower to do their own due diligence.

You will need to have an attorney to draw up the documents, and it's important that the attorney practices in the state where the property is located. More about that later. There are also some documents you need to have to protect the interests of both parties. These include at a minimum:

- Mortgage or deed of trust
- Promissory note
- Property insurance policy naming you as an additional insured

Some of the other necessary documents are a *Personal Guarantee*, pictures of the property and a scope of work to be done on the property. As a private lender, you could have your own requirements in addition to those mentioned above. Here are a few more questions you can ask as part of your preliminary screening as a prospective borrower.

- Will my money be in first position?
- How many other lenders will be loaning money on this property?
- How much of your own money will you be putting into this deal?

Again, whether lender or borrower, neither of you wants to become a victim of fraud. We routinely hear about individuals who invested their earnings or life savings into a property with an investor who promised them a quick, massive return on their money. The news accounts make it appear that those people just carried a bag of money into an alley and handed it over to someone without any questions asked. If they had gotten the above-mentioned documents, then fraud would have been *less* likely.

Remember, there is some risk in every investment. That's why we have the Securities and Exchange Commission (SEC). Their role is to regulate stocks, bonds and other investments to protect consumers. The SEC has regulations regarding private money, like pooling money from several individuals, soliciting across state lines, guaranteeing a return and many more. If you are going to do any private money lending or borrowing, I would suggest that you at least become familiar with the SEC regulations so you can protect your investment.

I mentioned earlier that you need an attorney to draw up the paperwork in the state where the property is located. If the loan is not repaid and the lender must foreclose, the foreclosure process will be more efficient. Foreclosure laws and processes vary from state to state. As of today's date, in 2025 the average foreclosure takes in excess of 670 days, nearly two years. Depending on the state, the foreclosure process can be measured in years.

Private money can help you grow your real estate investment business exponentially. I've used private money a few times over the years, and my lenders were thrilled with the rate of return that they received on their money. Everyone should be having conversations, networking, and talking with friends, family, and people that we know to find out if they have some IRA money or 401K money that's sitting there and not drawing very much interest. You can give them an opportunity to put their money to work earning a greater return on their money.

HARD MONEY LENDING

The term *hard money* is a weird term that most people have never heard before. A hard money lender will loan money based on the hard asset (the property) itself. Hard money lenders will typically lend up to 65-70% of the after-repair value (ARV) of a property. The property is used as collateral and the borrower will receive the loan payments in draws only after certain parts of the project are completed. Therefore, the borrower will need some funds of their own to pay subcontractors and materials until they receive each draw. Here are some of the pros and cons of hard money.

Typical Terms:

- **12–15% Interest**
- **2–5 Points Upfront**
- Short-term (6–12 months)

Hard money is fast but expensive. It's great for flips or short-term holds. But always have a clear exit strategy: refinance, sell, or transition to long-term financing.

Pros:

- Quick approvals (24–48 hours)
- No income verification
- Based on the asset value

Cons:

- High interest and fees
- Short payback period

While hard money lenders will pull credit reports, the quality of credit is not the critical determining factor as it is with traditional loans. However, hard money lenders generally prefer not to work with inexperienced rehabbers. If you are a novice investor, it's wise to partner with an experienced rehabber before approaching a hard money lender. After you have a few deals under your belt, the lenders will be practically throwing money at you. Their rates will usually get better as you do more deals with them, and they become more comfortable with you.

It pays to understand the jargon used by hard money lenders. Let's say you call up a hard money lender and ask, "What are your interest rates?" They respond by saying, "We will lend up to 70% at 5/15 up to 6 months." The lender is saying that they will lend up to 70% ARV at 5 points and 15% interest. Each point is 1% of the loan which can be paid upfront or when the loan is paid off. Of course, the number 15 means a 15% interest rate. Now before you start to scream "highway robbery or bloody murder," just remember that the 15% interest is simple interest.

Let's consider an example: suppose you want to buy a property for $40,000 with an ARV of $100,000. In this case, the lender would provide up to $70,000, which should cover both the purchase price and the necessary renovations without requiring any of your own money. The typical hard-money loan is for six months, but it will also have an extension clause that will allow you to renew the loan for longer than six months. The key to using hard money is to get in and get the property fixed up and sold as quickly as possible. If you don't plan to sell and wish to hold for long-term rental, the lender will work to make sure that you have a refinance lender in place before lending you the money.

Personally, I have never used hard money, but I've known a few investors who jumpstarted their fix and flip businesses starting with hard money. After their businesses were up and running, they switched over to private money because hard money can be expensive. Some continue to use hard money occasionally if their funds are tapped out.

WHY I RECOMMEND SMALL LOCAL BANKS AND CREDIT UNIONS

When it comes to dealing with lending institutions, I only work with small local banks and credit unions. The reason for this preference is that these institutions are usually portfolio lenders. That means that when they make a mortgage loan to you, that loan stays at the bank and is not sold to another lender or institution. If you apply for a mortgage at a national bank or a large regional bank, that loan has to comply with Fannie Mae (FNMA) standards because the bank's intention is not to keep that loan in-house. Their intention is to sell that mortgage somewhere around the world. It's not unusual to close on a loan and within a few months receive a letter stating that you will start sending your mortgage payment to another bank. For example, I've had my personal home mortgage sold four or five times over the past 20 years.

I do my best to avoid the large national banks. They can be your best friend when things are going well and your biggest nightmare when things are not going well. Just seek out portfolio lenders and stick with them where possible. Another disadvantage of the larger national banks with Fannie Mae loans is that they will only allow you to have 4 mortgage loans in your name. Being limited to 4 mortgages is not much at all if you are an investor trying to build a rental portfolio.

In contrast, portfolio lenders typically do not impose a cap on the number of mortgages you can have in your name at any given time. While they may have a dollar limit across all loans at their bank, you can have as many individual mortgages as you wish, as long as you stay within that overall lending cap. This flexibility gives portfolio lenders a significant advantage over national banks.

I have used small local banks and credit unions over the years to help build my rental portfolio. They understand the local market and are usually a bit more flexible with their underwriting. When working with a good portfolio lender, the sky's the limit. You can own as many financed properties as you wish, and they will finance as many properties as you can bring to them. See the chart below with a comparison of funding choices.

Funding Source Comparison

Funding Source	Interest Rate	Credit Check?	Down Payment	Closing Speed	Negotiable Terms
Owner Financing	0% – 6% + (negotiable)	No	Negotiable	Fast (as quick as you want)	Fully negotiable
Private Money	6–12% +	Rarely	Often none	Very fast	Highly negotiable
Hard Money	12–15% + points	Light	Yes	1–5 days	Limited flexibility
Local Banks	Varies	Yes	10–20%	30–45 days	Some flexibility
National Banks	Varies	Yes	5–20%	45–60 days	Not negotiable

There is **always** a way to fund a good deal. Learn how each source works, practice your pitch, and most importantly, don't assume you can't do a deal just because you don't have the cash.

Creative investors solve problems!

Chapter 13:

OPERATE OUTSIDE OF YOUR COMFORT ZONE

We all have the same 24 hours a day. How you choose to spend your time is the only difference. My first step was making time to pursue my real estate dreams. To do that, I needed to understand how I was spending my time outside of work. I created a "life calendar" and mapped out my priorities: family time, physical and mental fitness, and time for real estate.

I carved out 24 hours each week—mostly during nights and weekends—specifically for working on real estate. That did not include the hours spent listening to CDs, audiobooks, and podcasts while driving. If you're keeping track of your time spent on various activities (life calendar), I would suggest you reevaluate your calendar at least quarterly because human nature causes us to gravitate away from those things that we like least, and towards those things we like more. I looked at my life calendar after about a year and realized that I was spending an average of 38 hours a week on real estate. The extra time came at the expense of my fitness goals, as I had started using workout time for real estate. This taught me an important lesson: **you must maintain balance in your life**. If you want to be a high achiever and truly happy, you can't risk your health or neglect your family just to build wealth. You don't want to reach the top, only to realize you sacrificed too much to enjoy it.

I've always been a reader, but I started reading even more books. I read any book that had *real estate* or a *millionaire* in the title. Most of the investors that I meet tell me that they got their start by reading Robert Kiyosaki's book, *Rich Dad, Poor Dad.* It was Kiyosaki who explained in plain English, how and why the wealthy become wealthy.

He drove home the point that W2 earners pay taxes first and then get to take home what's left. But business owners and real estate investors pay themselves first and pay taxes last. We both are taxed by the same US government, but business owners are taxed differently. Think of it this way, W2 earners call him "Uncle Sam." Do you recall as a child when you were playing with someone, and they would twist your arm and make you say "Uncle?" When you say uncle, that means surrender. Business owners, on the other hand, see Uncle Sam more as a "silent partner" who takes his share only after the business has been paid.

I encourage you – NO, I'm telling you to get out of your comfort zone now!

I've explained to you how I made money in real estate. Further, I have chronicled my real estate experiences and laid out a guide that you can follow to get started investing in real estate today.

I never said any of this would be easy. However, if you are consistently persistent in your pursuit of real estate wealth. You can apply the principles and techniques that I laid out in this book and someday achieve your financial dreams in real estate just as I have done.

One of the main reasons this book was written is to take away all of your excuses. When I say *all* excuses, I mean ALL excuses. We can easily allow that self-pity to creep in and start to think of ourselves as something less. Nope! Nope, not on my watch!

I draw inspiration from reading biographies and autobiographies of individuals who display the bootstrapper mentality and refuse to let circumstance stop them from achieving. I've read literally dozens of books about successful people who started with nothing and became high achievers.

One individual that you've probably heard of is R. David Thomas, founder of Wendy's Restaurants. Dave was adopted as an infant and his adopted mother died, leaving him an orphan at the age of 4 years old. Those humble beginnings didn't stop Dave from building one of the largest hamburger restaurant chains with over 6,000 stores in America.

Another bootstrapper, Maggie L. Walker of Richmond, Virginia, lost her father at the age of 12. She and her mother washed clothes for neighbors to earn a living and pay for schooling. Maggie L, Walker went on to become the first African American woman to establish a bank in the United States—Saint Luke Penny Savings Bank in Richmond, VA.

Could you imagine having to struggle like Authur "A. G." Gaston, born near Birmingham Alabama in the late 1800s. He went from working in a coal mine earning pennies a day to owning numerous businesses including a hotel, funeral home, construction company, radio stations and several more. In 1996 at the time of his death his net worth was estimated at $130 million dollars.

There is no shortage of people who have achieved well beyond their perceived limits as set by others. To close out this inspirational chapter, I'm going to share with you the success stories of three more entrepreneurs. I chose to write about them because they are in my world. When I say in my world, it means that I have personally met them and have drawn inspiration from them for decades.

They all started out as ordinary people and, in most instances, less than ordinary people and they achieved extraordinary results. When I say, less than ordinary, some of them started with situations that could have been perceived by others as a handicap. However, these individuals persisted and did not allow other people's impressions of them to stop them from achieving.

MEET THREE MORE CONSISTENTLY PERSISTENT INDIVIDUALS WHO WOULD NOT QUIT

To achieve your goals, you must be consistently persistent, you must desire something so strongly that failure is not an option. Here, I want to highlight three individuals who embodied the bootstrapper mentality. They started with nothing, created a plan, and worked relentlessly to achieve success.

First, let's talk about one of the most recognized motivational speakers in the world: **Les Brown**. For over 15 years, I listened to Les Brown every single day of my life. I had his cassette tape series *Live Your Dreams* that I played on my radio cassette player that I kept on the nightstand by my bed. That old cassette player was always chewing up my cassette. I remember having to cut and splice those tapes back together dozens of times until that cassette player finally chewed up the entire cassette. I eventually had to retire that old cassette player.

I did have the pleasure of meeting Les Brown back in 2005 when he gave a three-hour presentation in Raleigh, North Carolina. Imagine this: a man abandoned at birth, labeled developmentally delayed, held back in school—how does someone with that background become a state legislator, one of the top five speakers in the world, and command over $25,000 for a single hour of speaking? Les overcame tremendous odds to excel in the speaking industry. I still listen to his speeches for motivation even today and I get excited when I hear him say "you got to be hungry!"

Another major motivator in my early entrepreneurial days was **Dr. Joe L. Dudley Sr.**, owner of Dudley Beauty Products in Greensboro, North Carolina. Mr. Dudley was the first millionaire I ever met. I met him when he was hosting monthly study groups for us aspiring entrepreneurs. I remember driving to Greensboro, NC, on Tuesday nights to attend discussions about business success principles and read books about successful businesspeople. Mr. Dudley was a multi-millionaire at the time, and it truly amazed me that he was so humble and giving of his time and wisdom to inspire us young entrepreneurs. I vividly recall Mr. Dudley saying that "reading people are ruling people." He read every day of his life, and he instilled reading in us and everyone around him.

He was born anything but a millionaire. Raised on a small farm in a community in rural eastern North Carolina, he was one of 10 children. His family of 12 lived in a cramped, four-room house, and times were tough. Mr. Dudley also struggled with stuttering and had academic difficulties throughout school. But in the 9th grade, after an encounter with another student, something changed. He decided to go back and read all his old textbooks, starting from the first grade and working his way up until he reached grade level. That determination led him to attend and graduate from North Carolina A&T State University.

He started his sales career as a door-to-door products salesman. Growing up during lean times prepared him for the lean times he faced in building his business. You would have to wonder how a person who grew up with a stutter could succeed in door-to-door selling. Mr. He often said, *"For every disadvantage, there is an equal or greater advantage."* His perceived disadvantage became his strength, as he consistently persisted. He knocked on doors daily, selling products during the day, and at night, he and his wife would wash and fill bottles to sell the next day. This relentless effort eventually built a multi-million-dollar business.

Prior to meeting Mr. Dudley, I still had this belief in the back of my mind that if someone is a millionaire they must have stolen, swindled, or taken advantage of some less fortunate people to obtain their money. It went along with the scarcity mentality that a lot of us carry with us even today. We sometimes carry the limiting belief that only special people will ever be wealthy. The feeling is that no matter how hard you try it will never happen to you. I always say just do what wealthy people did to become wealthy and ultimately you too will become wealthy. I realized that wealthy people start with a vision; they develop a plan, and they go to work. They focus on their vision and work on their plan every day until they succeed. I won't say that they never think about failing, they view failing "very expensive tuition." They don't dwell on failing and they never view themselves as a failure.

Sadly, during the writing of this book, I learned of Mr. Dudley's passing. He was an incredible asset to the Greensboro, NC community, to his alma mater, North Carolina Agricultural & Technical State University, and to all who knew him. Mr. Dudley will be deeply missed.

Finally, I recall a schoolmate of mine from my college days at Elizabeth City State University in Elizabeth City, N.C. Charles "Charlie" Hardesty was an Industrial Arts major, and I was an Industrial Technology major. I tutored him in drafting, and we both played on the football team together where he played quarterback.

Charles "Charlie" Hardesty, Winston Salem, NC

It was my understanding that Charlie came from humble beginnings in Beaufort, NC. The last time we had seen each other was in 1977. I had often wondered what happened to Charlie since our school days.

Nearly 20 years later, in 1996, I unexpectedly ran into Charlie at a basketball tournament in Winston-Salem, NC. He was standing casually along the wall, as unassuming as ever. We shook hands and spent time reminiscing about old times. I asked him, "So, Charlie, what are you up to now?" "Oh, I own a small fish market across town," he replied. "Swing by after the games and grab some fresh fried fish."

The next day, I stopped by, and there he was, the proud owner of Forsyth Seafood in Winston-Salem, NC. I asked him how he'd managed to rise from humble beginnings in rural eastern North Carolina to build a business capable of creating generational wealth for his family.

Charlie told me his story, and it was then that I realized that he was a true bootstrapper, someone who had gone well beyond his comfort zone and my expectations of him. After moving to Winston-Salem, Charlie worked at a small warehouse and started a side hustle buying fresh seafood from the coast and selling it locally. His dedication was astonishing—he commuted nearly five hours each way to the coast to purchase seafood, then sold it in the city. For years, he built a solid reputation for selling quality products, saving all his earnings from his side hustle.

Then when the opportunity came to buy his own fish market and seafood restaurant, he was able to take full advantage of it. I was so proud to see that Charles "Charlie" Hardesty had succeeded against the odds and was now creating generational wealth for his family. Every time I went to Winston Salem I would stop by for a visit, and we would reminisce about old times. Sometimes we would spend hours just talking about business. He would always offer me a free meal, which I gladly accepted.

Sadly, Charlie passed away in 2013. He was posthumously recognized by the City of Winston Salem, N.C., by having a street named in his honor. The street is named Hardesty Lane in Winston Salem, N.C. Charlie was a loyal friend, dedicated to his alma mater and his community until the end. His story remains an inspiring example of perseverance and the power of side hustles in creating generational wealth.

You too can persevere and achieve just like the above-mentioned individuals if you decide what you want, develop a plan and JUST GO TO WORK!

Chapter 14:

WHEN LIFE GIVES YOU LEMONS

Elbert Hubbard is credited with coining the phrase "when life gives you lemons, make lemonade." It's a proverb that encourages a positive mental attitude and optimism in the face of adversity.

If life gave me lemons, I would make as much lemonade as I could. Then I would find others to share the lemonade with. We would sit there sipping lemonade and engaging in casual lively conversations, with a little bit of humor and lots of education and inspiration.

I would provide you with seeds so you can plant your own trees, harvest your own lemons, and make your own lemonade. In turn, I would ask each of you to go out and share your lemonade, education and inspiration with others. Before we know it, we will have shared lemonade with the entire world.

That's just what I've attempted to do by writing this book. I poured a lot of my 25 plus years of real estate education, experiences, and applied knowledge into this text. This book was written to shorten your learning curve allowing you to pick up this book and start making money in real estate immediately. You can do just that. I used this knowledge to buy properties to supplement my income while still working a day job. You may wish to build a huge portfolio of properties, quit your day job and retire young. Then there are others who might want to use their income from real estate investment to jump start another business venture. It's up to you to use real estate as your wealth creation tool to take you wherever you want to go.

Just like being handed lemons, take this information, read it, share it and take action. I know this book is not for everybody. But I would be highly disappointed if you read this entire book and didn't take any action whatsoever. If you read this book and decide that it's not for you, then pass it on to someone else. Someone would be glad if you decided to share a glass of lemonade.

I'll see you at the closing table!

GLOSSARY

Administrator

A person appointed by a court to manage the estate of a deceased individual who did not leave a valid will (intestate).

Administrator (Alternative Definition)

In some contexts, this term can also refer to an individual responsible for managing and overseeing the administration of a trust or estate.

After Repair Value (ARV)

The estimated value of a property after it has been renovated or repaired. Often used in the context of fixing and flipping homes.

Amortization Table

A schedule of payments detailing the amount of principal and interest that will be paid over the life of a loan, typically for a mortgage.

Assignee

A person or entity to whom rights, interests, or obligations under a contract or agreement are transferred.

Assignor

A person or entity that transfers their rights, interests, or obligations under a contract to another party (the assignee).

Assignment

The transfer of rights or interests from one party (the assignor) to another party (the assignee). Common in real estate contracts and assignments of lease.

Balloon Payment

A large payment due at the end of a loan term, after smaller periodic payments have been made. Often used in short-term loans.

Bandit Sign

Informal marketing signs typically posted in public areas, often used to advertise real estate investment services (e.g., "I Buy Houses").

Bootstrapper

An investor who builds their portfolio with minimal external capital, leveraging creativity, sweat equity, and strategic reinvestment.

Cash Out

Refers to pulling equity out of a property, usually through refinancing or selling, to access liquid cash.

Closing

The final step in a real estate transaction where ownership is transferred from the seller to the buyer, and all financial and legal documents are finalized.

Closing Statement

A document that outlines the final financial details of a real estate transaction, including the buyer's and seller's costs and credits. It is often referred to as a HUD-1 statement in real estate transactions involving a loan.

Comparable Sales (Comps)

Properties similar to a subject property that have recently sold. Used to help determine the market value of a property.

Compound Interest

Interest that is calculated on both the initial principal and the accumulated interest from previous periods.

Consideration

The value exchanged in a contract. In real estate, this typically refers to the price a buyer agrees to pay for a property.

Contract

A legally binding agreement between two or more parties that outlines the terms of a transaction, such as the sale of real estate.

Contract Assignment

The process of transferring the rights and obligations of a contract from one party (assignor) to another (assignee), often used in wholesale real estate deals.

Contract for Deed

A form of seller financing where the seller retains legal title to the property until the buyer has paid off the full purchase price, at which point title is transferred to the buyer.

Deed

A legal document that transfers ownership of real property from one party to another.

Deed of Trust

A type of secured real estate loan where the borrower conveys title to a third-party trustee until the debt is paid off.

Deficiency Judgment

A court order that requires a borrower to pay the difference between the sale price of a property at foreclosure and the outstanding mortgage balance.

Dodd-Frank

The Dodd-Frank Wall Street Reform and Consumer Protection Act, created the Consumer Financial Protection Bureau (CFPB) to oversee consumer protection in financial transactions, including mortgage lending. The law introduced stricter lending standards and transparency requirements for financial institutions and mortgage servicers.

Double Close

A strategy where an investor buys and then immediately resells a property in two separate transactions. The investor does not take title to the property, but the deal is structured as two closings.

Due-On-Sale Clause

A provision in a mortgage or deed of trust that requires the borrower to pay off the entire loan balance if the property is sold or transferred.

Earnest Money Deposit (EMD)

A deposit made by a buyer to demonstrate their commitment to a transaction. It is held in escrow and applied to the purchase price or returned if the deal falls through under certain conditions.

Escrow

A neutral third party that holds funds or documents related to a real estate transaction until certain conditions are met, such as completing a sale.

FANNIE MAE (Federal National Mortgage Association)
A government-sponsored enterprise that provides liquidity to the mortgage market by buying and guaranteeing loans from lenders, primarily on conforming loans.

FREDDIE MAC (Federal Home Loan Mortgage Corporation)
A government-sponsored enterprise similar to Fannie Mae but primarily focused on purchasing and guaranteeing mortgages on single-family homes and multi-family properties.

Fair Market Value (FMV)
The price at which a property would sell in an open and competitive market, assuming both the buyer and seller have reasonable knowledge of the property and no undue pressure to buy or sell.

FHA Loan (Federal Housing Administration Loan)
A type of government-backed mortgage designed to help low-to moderate-income buyers purchase homes with a smaller down payment.

First Mortgage
The primary loan on a property that has first claim on the asset in the event of default or foreclosure.

FNMA (Fannie Mae)
See "Fannie Mae."

Hard Money
Short-term loans typically secured by real estate and provided by private investors or companies, often used for property acquisitions or flips. These loans are based on the value of the property rather than the borrower's creditworthiness.

Hard Money Loan

A loan that is secured by real estate and funded by private lenders. These loans generally have higher interest rates and shorter terms than conventional loans.

Hard Money Lender

A private individual or company that provides hard money loans, typically for real estate investment purposes.

Heir

A person legally entitled to inherit property or assets from a deceased individual, often under the terms of a will or through intestate succession.

Heirs

The plural form of heir, referring to multiple individuals who are entitled to inherit a deceased person's estate.

House Hacking

An investing strategy where you live in part of a property (like a duplex or fourplex) while renting out the other units to offset living expenses.

HUD-1

A standardized form used in real estate transactions to itemize the costs associated with closing, including fees for both the buyer and the seller. It is often replaced by the Closing Disclosure for most residential transactions after 2015.

Intestate

The condition of dying without a valid will. In such cases, the state determines how the deceased's property will be distributed.

Judicial Foreclosure

A legal process in which a lender files a lawsuit in court to foreclose on a property, often requiring a judicial ruling before the property can be sold to satisfy the loan.

Land Contract

A type of seller financing where the buyer makes payments directly to the seller in exchange for the property, and the seller retains legal title until the full purchase price is paid.

Landlord

A property owner who leases or rents out real estate to tenants in exchange for rent payments.

Lease Option

A contract that gives a tenant the right to purchase the leased property at a later date, typically at a predetermined price.

Lease to Own

An arrangement where a tenant rents a property with the option or agreement to purchase it at a later date, usually with part of the rent paid going toward the purchase price.

Lessee

The tenant in a lease agreement who rents the property.

Lessor

The property owner or landlord in a lease agreement.

Lien

A legal claim or encumbrance on a property as collateral for a debt or obligation.

Lis Pendens
A notice filed with the county recording office that indicates a legal action is pending concerning a property, often related to a foreclosure or dispute over ownership.

Master Lease
A lease agreement in which the lessee gains control of a property and may sublease it to others, often used in creative investing.

Maximum Allowable Offer (MAO)
The highest price an investor is willing to pay for a property, based on its after-repair value and estimated renovation costs.

Mid-term rental
A rental arrangement lasting between 1–6 months, often catering to travel nurses, remote workers, or temporary relocations.

Mortgagee
The lender or institution that provides a mortgage loan.

Mortgage Position
Refers to the order of lien priority on a property, determining which lender gets paid first in a foreclosure.

Mortgagor
The borrower who takes out a mortgage loan to purchase a property.

Multiple Listing Service (MLS)
A database used by real estate brokers to list properties for sale and to share information about available properties.

National REIA

The National Real Estate Investors Association, a trade organization that supports real estate investors through education, networking, and resources.

Option Contract

A contract that grants the buyer the right, but not the obligation, to purchase a property at a predetermined price within a specified time frame.

Optionee

The person who holds the right to buy in an option contract.

Optionor

The property owner who grants the option to buy.

P & I (Principal and Interest)

The portion of a monthly mortgage payment that goes toward paying off the loan balance (principal) and interest charges.

Performance Lease

A lease agreement based on the performance of a business, often used in commercial real estate, where rent may be tied to revenue.

PITI (Principal, Interest, Taxes, Insurance)

The total monthly mortgage payment, including principal and interest on the loan, property taxes, and homeowners insurance.

Points (Mortgage Points)

Fees paid to the lender at closing, often expressed as a percentage of the loan amount. Each point typically represents 1% of the loan amount.

Portfolio Loan

A loan that is made by a lender and held in their portfolio, rather than being sold on the secondary market. Portfolio loans are often more flexible in terms of requirements.

Principal

The original loan amount borrowed or the remaining balance on a loan, excluding interest.

Private Money

Loans provided by private individuals or groups (as opposed to institutional lenders) to fund real estate investments, often at higher interest rates.

Proof of Funds

A document or bank statement provided by a buyer to show they have the necessary cash available to close on a real estate transaction. Often required in competitive or cash-only deals.

Purchase Agreement

A legally binding contract between a buyer and seller outlining the terms and conditions of a real estate transaction.

Purchase and Sale Agreement

Another term for the purchase agreement; it formalizes the terms and conditions under which the buyer agrees to purchase, and the seller agrees to sell the property.

Rehabber

A real estate investor who purchases properties in need of repair or renovation, renovates them, and then sells them for a profit.

Rental Arbitrage

A strategy where an investor leases a property long-term and re-rents it short-term (e.g., on Airbnb), profiting from the spread.

Right of Redemption

The legal right of a borrower to reclaim a foreclosed property by paying off the loan balance, including any accrued fees and interest, within a specified period.

Sandwich Lease Option

An investing strategy where an investor leases a property with the option to buy, then subleases it with another lease-option to a tenant-buyer, profiting from the spread.

Securities and Exchange Commission (SEC)

A federal agency that regulates the sale of securities, including certain real estate investments like syndications and REITs.

Short term rental

A rental property leased for short stays, typically under 30 days, through platforms like Airbnb or VRBO.

Second Mortgage

A subordinate loan taken out in addition to the first mortgage, typically at a higher interest rate and with more risk.

Simple Interest

Interest that is calculated only on the principal amount of a loan or investment, without compounding. Simple interest is typically used in short-term loans and is easier to calculate than compound interest.

Strike Price

The agreed-upon purchase price in an option contract, which the optionee can exercise within a specified time frame.

Subject-to

A real estate investment strategy where an investor acquires a property "Subject-to" the existing financing, meaning the original mortgage stays in place, and the buyer takes ownership without formally assuming the loan.

Terms

The specific conditions and provisions outlined in a contract, agreement, or loan, including the payment schedule, interest rate, length of the agreement, and any other clauses that define the relationship between the parties involved.

Tiny house

A small, often mobile, home under 500 square feet—used for minimal living or as an affordable housing or rental investment.

Title Company

A company that specializes in verifying and insuring titles to real estate. They ensure that the property title is clear of liens or other encumbrances before the sale and issue title insurance to protect buyers and lenders from title defects.

Transactional Funding

Short-term, high-interest funding, used by real estate investors to quickly close deals, often for a "double close" transaction. The funding is typically provided for just a few days and is used to bridge the gap between the purchase and resale of a property.

Wholesaler

A real estate investor who finds properties at a deep discount and contracts them for sale to other investors. The wholesaler typically doesn't take possession of the property but assigns the contract to another buyer for a fee.

www.ingramcontent.com/pod-product-compliance
Lightning Source LLC
Chambersburg PA
CBHW071744120626

46550CB00002B/661

* 9 7 9 8 8 9 3 7 9 5 6 9 1 *